AF735535

Labour Law in Singapore

Labour Law in Singapore

Ravi Chandran

This book was originally published as a monograph in the International Encyclopaedia of Laws/Labour Law and Industrial Relations.

Founding Editor: Roger Blanpain
General Editor: Frank Hendrickx
Volume Editor: Frank Hendrickx

Wolters Kluwer

Published by:
Kluwer Law International B.V.
PO Box 316
2400 AH Alphen aan den Rijn
The Netherlands
E-mail: international-sales@wolterskluwer.com
Website: lrus.wolterskluwer.com

Sold and distributed by:
Wolters Kluwer Legal & Regulatory U.S.
7201 McKinney Circle
Frederick, MD 21704
United States of America
E-mail: customer.service@wolterskluwer.com

ISBN 978-94-035-3685-9

e-Book: ISBN 978-94-035-3690-3
web-PDF: ISBN 978-94-035-3691-0

The Author

Ravi Chandran graduated from the Faculty of Law, the National University of Singapore, in 1991. He did his pupilage at Messers Lee and Lee and was called to the Bar in 1992. He was in private practice for some time before he set off to do his Masters in Law at Queen's College, Cambridge University. He returned in 1995 and since then has been teaching in the School of Business, National University of Singapore. He teaches various subjects, including Employment Law. He has published widely in the area of Employment Law, both locally and internationally, and his work has been cited in court judgments, books and journal articles. His opinion on Employment Law matters has been sought by, among others, law firms, government-linked organizations and the International Labour Organization. He was also the former President of the Asian Society of Labour Law Scholars.

The Author

Table of Contents

List of Abbreviations

MLJ	*Malayan Law Journal*
SLR	Singapore Law Reports
SLR (R)	Singapore Law Reports (Reissue)
SSLR	Straits Settlements Law Reports

List of Abbreviations

General Introduction

Chapter 1. General Background

§1. Geography

1. Singapore is a small country in Southeast Asia. It is made up of sixty-three islands, including the main island. It is separated from Malaysia in the north by the Straits of Johor, and it is separated from the Riau Islands of Indonesia in the south by the Singapore Straits. Singapore in the past had a land area of over 500 square kilometres, but now through the process of land reclamation, it stretches over 700 square kilometres. Being a small country makes it easy to enforce laws effectively, including those relating to employment, such as the laws on health and safety and the illegal employment of foreign workers.

§2. Population

2. As of 2020, Singapore has a population of about 5.69 million, the vast bulk of whom live on the main island. Of the population, about 30% is made up of foreigners, that is, non-citizens and non-permanent residents. Thus, there is a high percentage of foreigners in Singapore. In terms of ethnic make-up, the Chinese make up roughly about 76% of the population and are the majority. Malays make up about 15%, Indians about 7% and others about 2% of the population. These figures are correct as of 2019. The increasing presence of foreigners in Singapore is part of the government's strategy to deal with the rapidly ageing local population and declining birth rates. The presence of a large foreign work force also has implications in the field of employment law and industrial relations. For instance, after twenty-six years of being strike free, Singapore faced a strike in 2012 by a group of foreign bus drivers who were not aware of or familiar with local laws.

§3. Political and Judicial System

3. Singapore is a republic, and executive power is vested in the cabinet headed by the Prime Minister. It follows a unicameral system. Parliamentary elections have to be held within three months of the dissolution of Parliament, which would normally happen every five years.[1] The People's Action Party has won every election since self-governance was granted in 1959, completely or by a vast majority. Singapore also has an elected President, elections for whom are held every six years.[2] Though the President has some important powers, the President's role is largely ceremonial. Since Singapore is largely governed by one party, this makes it easy for laws, including employment laws, to be passed quickly to deal with issues that may be a pressing concern for society, such as health and safety at work or declining birth rates which may be due to maternity benefits not being attractive enough.

4. The Constitution of Singapore, which is the supreme law of the country,[3] came into effect on 9 August 1965, and it lays down the powers of the three organs of State, namely the legislature, the executive and the judiciary. It also provides for other matters such as fundamental liberties. Though the Constitution is the supreme law of the country, thus far, as a matter of practice, it has had little impact in the field of employment law other than in a few instances relating to the dismissal of public servants.[4]

5. In terms of the legal system, having been a British colony, Singapore follows the common law system, whereby besides written laws, judge-made laws can act as binding precedents. In relation to the field of employment law, there are many written laws that will be referred to later. However, there is also a huge body of judge-made case law governing various aspects of employment. It should also be highlighted that Singapore abolished the jury system in 1970 and that the Court of Appeal is the highest court in Singapore.

§4. Employment Statistics

6. In Singapore, there is good participation in employment by people of both sexes. In 1970, about 81% of the males were in the workforce compared to 28% of the females. In 2020, the percentage of males in the workforce was about 75%, while that of females increased to about 61%. This trend is likely to continue well into the future. Increased female employment could be one factor that has contributed to declining birth rates. To address this issue, the government has taken a multi-pronged approach, including enacting specific employment-related laws to provide incentives for procreation.

7. Unemployment rates in Singapore are generally low. In more recent times, it has hovered around slightly over 2% with the exception of some years such as 2002, 2003, 2004, 2005, 2009 and 2020 when it was above 3%. Many policies contribute

1. Articles 65 and 66 of the Constitution of the Republic of Singapore.
2. Article 20 of the Constitution of the Republic of Singapore.
3. Article 4 of the Constitution of the Republic of Singapore.
4. *See*, for instance, Art. 110(3) of the Constitution and *Attorney-General, Singapore v. Lee Keng Kee* [1981–1982] SLR (R) 460.

to the low unemployment figures, including the provision of subsidized training schemes which allow employees to upgrade their skills and remain employable and employment laws that are not overly burdensome on employers, which could have helped businesses to stay afloat in a highly competitive global environment, thereby not having to retrench employees.

§5. Social and Cultural Values

8. Singapore has a diverse culture with several languages spoken, and religions practised. Nonetheless, by and large, Singapore society is conservative and law-abiding. However, as it evolves, things are slowly changing, especially among the younger members of the population. This has further accelerated with the growth of the Internet and social media. All this could have an impact on the development of employment law in Singapore in the years to come.

Chapter 2. Definitions and Notions

§1. Labour Law and Social Security Law

9. In Singapore, there are various statutes providing some form of social security, such as the Central Provident Fund Act and the Work Injury Compensation Act. The government too has various forms of social assistance schemes in place, some of which are highlighted in this work. However, given that Singapore is a very small country, there is no significant distinction between labour law and social security law in terms of practitioners or dispute resolution mechanisms. As such, no distinction will be made between the two in this work.

§2. Categories of Employee

10. Singapore has several statutes governing employment, though the most important one is the Employment Act which lays down various rights and obligations. However, the Employment Act does not apply to all employees. Pursuant to section 2(1) of the Employment Act, the following employees are excluded: seafarers and domestic workers. Further, section 2(1) provides that the President may make declarations as to the class of government employees who are covered under the Employment Act. However, to date, no such declaration has been made, and hence government employees are not covered. On the other hand, section 2(1) of the Employment Act allows the Minister of Manpower by declaration to exclude any categories of employees, and such a declaration has been issued to exclude statutory board employee, and hence employees of statutory boards are not covered. Before the amendments in 2018, not all executives and managers were covered by the Employment Act. However, following that amendment, all executives and managers are now covered, and this is a significant change.

11. The definition of the term 'domestic worker' in section 2(1) of the Employment Act includes motor car drivers or chauffeurs. The reason why seafarers and domestic workers are excluded is due to the nature of their duties, though there have been some recent calls for domestic workers to be included in the legislation. As for government and statutory board employees, though they are excluded from the ambit of the Employment Act, as a matter of practice, they do enjoy similar or even better terms or benefits.

12. The Employment Act only applies to 'employees', other than those excluded, as described in the preceding paragraph. Though the term 'employee' is defined in section 2(1) of the Employment Act, the definition is not clear, and hence reference has to be made to case law in determining who an employee is. In this regard, it is likely that no single factor is conclusive in determining who is an employee and all the relevant circumstances have to be taken into account.[5] Factors that could be relevant include matters such as the extent of control exercised by the person requesting the service, the method of payment involved, the types of benefits offered, the amount of restrictions imposed on the person providing the service, the provision of tools, equipment and other things such as uniforms by the person requesting the service and the extent to which the person providing the service bears any risk of making a loss or shares any chance of making a profit. Thus, for instance, temporary, freelance[6] or volunteer workers may or may not be employees, depending on such factors. The problem particularly arises when workers are hired through an employment agency. In such a situation, depending on such factors, it is possible that the worker is the employee of the client organization or of the employment agency or of neither. If a person is not deemed to be an employee, generally, he will not have any statutory rights relating to employment, unlike in some countries, where such persons may still have some statutory protection. However, as at the time of writing, the possibility of conferring some rights on some persons who are not employees is being explored.

13. However, once a person is an 'employee' and does not fall within the excluded categories discussed earlier, it does not matter whether he is a foreigner or only works on a part-time basis. Nonetheless, in relation to part-time employees, under section 66B of the Employment Act, the Minister has the power to make regulations to exclude or modify any or all of the provisions of that Act in their application to part-time employees, and such regulations have indeed been made,[7] the main effect of them being that most rights are pro-rated according to the amount of part-time work done.

14. The Employment Act also refers to 'workman', a term which is defined in section 2(1). Though the term 'workman' is defined in section 2(1), again, since the definition is not entirely clear, reference has to be made to case law. In this regard, it is likely that the term 'workman' refers to someone whose work is predominantly manual in nature, that is, predominantly involves the use of hands.[8] It may be important to determine whether an employee is a workman, as, under the Employment Act, a workman could be endowed with certain additional rights under Part IV of the Employment Act.

15. Besides the Employment Act, there are also distinctions between various types of workers under some other statutes.

For instance, under the Work Injury Compensation Act, by virtue of the Fourth Schedule to that Act, domestic workers and others such as members of the Singapore Armed Forces, Singapore Police Force and the Singapore Civil Defence Force are excluded. Though domestic workers are excluded, it must be highlighted

---

5. *See*, for instance, *Kureoka Enterprise Pte Ltd v. Central Provident Fund Board*, Suit No. 218 of 1991, Singapore High Court, unreported.
6. *Ibid.*
7. *See* Employment (Part-time Employees) Regulations.
8. *See*, for instance, *Hennedige Oliver v. Public Prosecutor* [1985–1986] SLR (R) 336.

that the bulk of domestic workers in Singapore are foreigners and under the work permit conditions[9] pursuant to which they are hired, employers have to take out compulsory insurance to cover eventualities such as death, though the potential amount of payout is lower. As for other categories of employees excluded, they are excluded as they are covered by other internal schemes which offer the same or better protection.

16. Another example would be the Central Provident Fund Act. By virtue of several orders[10] made under that Act, several sets of employees are excluded. For instance, domestic employees are excluded. Further, foreigners who are not Singapore citizens or permanent residents are excluded. The aim of the Central Provident Fund Act is to provide for an income stream upon retirement, and hence non-citizens and permanent residents who are not expected to retire in Singapore do not get the benefit of the scheme. Domestic workers are typically foreigners, and hence they too are excluded.

§3. Categories of Employer

17. As for the definition of 'employer', most statutes that impose obligations on employers define the term 'employer'. These include the Employment Act, the Work Injury Compensation Act and the Central Provident Fund Act. Most statutes would also include all categories of employers, though there are exceptions. For instance, under the Employment Act, since government and statutory board employees are excluded, the government and statutory boards do not owe obligations to employees under the Employment Act. Similarly, under the Personal Data Protection Act, by virtue of section 4 of that Act, public agencies such as the government and statutory boards do not owe duties under that Act, including to their employees.

18. In Singapore, generally, the types of statutory obligations of the employer do not vary according to the type of enterprise involved other than as stated in the preceding paragraph. Thus, for instance, whether it is a limited company with many employees or a sole proprietorship with just a few employees, generally, the same statutory obligations apply.

9. *See* para. 47.
10. *See* Central Provident Fund (Exemption – Foreign Employees) Order and Central Provident Fund (Exemptions – Miscellaneous) (Consolidation) Order.

Chapter 3. Role of Government

§1. Degree of Government Intervention

19. In Singapore, the government and government institutions (such as the Ministry of Manpower) play a very active role in the shaping, administration and enforcement of labour policies and laws.

Over the past decade, many new laws have been introduced and existing ones amended. For some of these laws, the push to introduce them may have come from unions or employees or even non-governmental organizations. For others, it may have come from the government itself. However, what has to be highlighted is that in Singapore, there is a system of tripartism that extends to the enactment of new laws as well. Each time a new labour law is to be passed, there is widespread consultation between the government, employers and employees or unions. Public consultations with members of the public are also typically sought. It is only after extensive consultations and after balancing all the competing interests that the relevant law sought to be tabled in Parliament.

20. It should also be highlighted that in respect of many labour laws, the final decision to enact them is based on factors such as practicality, the extent of the underlying problem which the law is trying to address, the cost impact on the employer if such laws were to be enacted and the availability of other alternatives. International obligations or expectations typically do not play a vital role in the development of new employment laws or the amendment of existing ones in Singapore.

§2. Income and Industrial Policy

21. The government is also, to some extent, involved in designing income policy through the auspices of the National Wages Council, which was set up in 1972. The National Wages Council meets annually to issue guidelines as to the way in which salaries should be adjusted based on general economic conditions. These guidelines are used as a basis for negotiation between the employer and unions. There is tripartite representation in the National Wages Council, and hence besides the government, there are representatives from employers and the unions as well. As a result of these national guidelines, wage increases or decreases are made in a more orderly and less combative manner, especially where unions are concerned.

22. In relation to industrial policy, the government plays an equally dominant role. Upon independence, there was huge unemployment. Thus, there was a need to attract foreign investment. However, Singapore had no natural resources to speak of. Thus the government felt that besides matters such as infrastructure upgrading and tax policies, one way in which foreign investors could be attracted to Singapore was if industrial relations were made harmonious. In order to accomplish this, various legislative changes were undertaken. The details surrounding Singapore's industrial relations system are discussed in Part II of this work.

§3. Competence of the Government and/or Ministries or Other Agencies

23. In general, the government, as well as the Ministry of Manpower and other agencies, are very proactive and are keen to find out what is happening on the ground and to address and solve labour issues and problems as they arise. For instance, in recent times, there has been a strong anti-foreigner sentiment among the local population, and in light of this, the employment policies relating to the hiring of foreign workers have been tightened. Besides enacting laws to address issues as they arise, laws that are so enacted are also generally strictly and effectively enforced.

Chapter 4. Sources of Labour Law

§1. Constitution and Legislation

24. As already mentioned, the Constitution is the supreme law of the country,[11] and it has some provisions which may relate to employment, such as discrimination.[12] Nonetheless, in Singapore, the role of the Constitution in the field of employment law has been limited as a matter of practice, other than in a few instances relating to the dismissal of public servants.[13]

25. In Singapore, there are also various statutes that impose obligations on the employer. These include the Employment Act, the Central Provident Fund Act, the Work Injury Compensation Act, the Workplace Safety and Health Act, the Retirement and Re-employment Act, the Industrial Relations Act, the Trade Unions Act and the Trade Disputes Act. Some of these statutes may also impose obligations on employees or unions, such as the Employment Act, the Workplace Safety and Health Act, the Industrial Relations Act, the Trade Unions Act and the Trade Disputes Act.

§2. Case Law and Other Sources

26. Being a common law country, another source of law is cases, and the doctrine of precedent is well entrenched in Singapore. There has been a steady stream of employment law-related cases dealing with diverse matters ranging from negligence to non-compete clauses, some of which are referred to in the course of this work.

27. Aside from statutes and cases, another source from which obligations can be imposed on the employer or employee is the individual contract of employment. Generally, a contract can be in writing or orally agreed to,[14] and it can have express terms or implied terms. Though a contract need not be in writing, if the employee falls under the Employment Act, the employer would have to provide the employee with key employment terms within fourteen days after the start of the employment, failing which the employer could face penalties.[15]

28. In relation to express terms, generally, they do not have to be fair in order to be binding, based on the doctrine of freedom of contract. However, there are a few exceptions. For instance, non-compete clauses may or may not be valid.[16] Similarly, it is possible for a statutory provision to provide that a certain right cannot be

11. Article 4 of the Constitution of the Republic of Singapore.
12. *See* para. 79.
13. *See*, for instance Art. 110(3) of the Constitution and *Attorney-General, Singapore v. Lee Keng Kee* [1981–1982] SLR (R) 460.
14. *See*, for instance, s. 2(1) of the Employment Act.
15. *See* s. 95A of the Employment Act.
16. *See* para. 212.

excluded by contract.[17] Aside from a few such exceptions, basically, the employer can impose whatever terms he wants, being in the stronger bargaining position.

29. In relation to implied terms, they can be implied on various grounds. First, they may be implied if they are so obvious that they go without saying and are necessary to give the contract business efficacy.[18] Terms are implied on this basis on the presumed intention of the parties and are known as terms implied by fact. Second, terms may be implied if the court considers it necessary that all contracts of that type should have such a standardized term. Terms are implied on this basis on the grounds of public policy rather than on the presumed intention of the parties and are known as terms implied by law. Third, terms may be implied by the past practice of the employer or the industry in question. However, as a matter of practice, very few terms are implied on this basis as usually to qualify as past practice or custom, the practice or custom must have gone on for a very long time.[19] Further, terms cannot be implied on any of the grounds discussed above if the effect is to contradict the express terms of the contract.[20]

30. Aside from the contract, where there is a union involved, the collective agreement could also impose obligations, typically on the employer. Such a collective agreement may be expressly included in individual contracts of employment. If it is, then the employee too can enforce it. If it is not, while the union can seek to enforce the collective agreement against the employer, an individual employee may not be able to directly enforce the collective agreement against the employer. This is so because the collective agreement represents a legally binding agreement only between the employer and the trade union.[21] As a matter of practice, there is unlikely to be a conflict between the terms of the collective agreement and the individual contract of employment as most employers would provide for the same benefits, even in the contracts of non-unionized workers. However, if the collective agreement is incorporated into the individual contract of employment and there is an inconsistency, as far as the employee is concerned, it is likely that the terms of the employment contract prevail, it being more specific to the employee.[22]

§3. Relationship Between the Different Sources of Law

31. As between the Constitution and statutes, should there be any inconsistency, the Constitution, being the supreme law of the country, prevails,[23] but such issues have seldom arisen in Singapore as a matter of practice in the area of employment law.

17. *See*, for instance, s. 86 of the Employment Act which relates to maternity leave.
18. *Ng Giap Hon v. Westcomb Securities Pte Ltd* [2009] 3 SLR (R) 518.
19. *D'cruz v. Seafield Amalgamated Rubber Co Ltd* [1963] MLJ 154.
20. *Loh Siok Wah v. American International Assurance Co Ltd* [1998] 2 SLR (R) 245.
21. Section 26 of the Industrial Relations Act.
22. *Aldabe Fermin v. Standard Chartered Bank* [2010] 3 SLR 722.
23. Article 4 of the Constitution of the Republic of Singapore.

32. In relation to the relationship between statutes on the one hand and collective agreements or contracts on the other, generally, statutes take precedence. Thus, generally, it is not possible to have a worse term than that guaranteed by a statute. However, there are some limited exceptions. For instance, under section 10(2) of the Employment Act, even though there is a period of notice provided for termination, the contract of employment can provide for a shorter period of notice. On the other hand, usually, the contract or the collective agreement can provide for better terms. However, again there are exceptions. For instance, section 48(3) of the Employment Act provides that any annual wage supplement cannot exceed one month. This is to encourage bonuses to be paid on the basis of performance and not as a matter of automatic entitlement.

§4. International Law

33. What has been discussed above relates to local sources. Another possible source of law could be international conventions, such as those promulgated by the International Labour Organization and ratified by Singapore. However, thus far, there have been no Singapore court cases in which an action has been based on an international convention that Singapore has ratified but for which there is no local legislation or in which an action has been based on the ground that some local legislation which is in existence is not in congruence with an international convention that Singapore has ratified.

Part I. The Individual Employment Relation

Chapter 1. Definitions and Concepts

34. Various statutes impose various obligations on the parties involved in an employment relationship. However, as mentioned previously, not all statutes impose obligations on all employers, and not all statutes apply to all employees. As this has already been discussed previously,[24] nothing more will be mentioned about this at this juncture.

24. *See* paras 10–18.

Chapter 2. Contract of Employment

§1. Essentials of a Contract

35. Subject to some very minor exceptions, a contract of employment may be written or orally agreed to.[25] Thus, generally, there is no requirement for contracts of employment to be in writing. Though a contract need not be in writing, if the employee falls under the Employment Act, the employer would have to provide the employee with key employment terms within fourteen days after the start of the employment, failing which the employer could face penalties.[26]

36. However, for there to be a valid contract, there must be an offer, an acceptance of that offer, consideration and an intention to create legal relations. In the employment context, typically, the employer will make an offer after an interview, and it will be up to the employee to accept or reject that offer. With an offer and acceptance, there will be an agreement, but in addition to that, there needs to be a consideration unless the contract is by seal or deed (which is not common in the employment context). The basic idea behind consideration is that each party to the contract must do or agree to do something in return for the other's promise. In the employment context, consideration on the part of the employer would be the provision of or the agreement to provide some form of remuneration such as salary and consideration on the part of the employee would be the provision of, or the agreement to provide, services. The final element necessary for there to be a valid contract is an intention to create legal relations on the part of both parties. This would usually be presumed in commercial transactions, which is the context in which employment contracts take place and hence this element would usually not pose a problem.

§2. Selection and Hiring

37. In terms of selection and hiring, it must be pointed out that Singapore does not have a general anti-discrimination law and has not ratified the International Labour Organization's Discrimination (Employment and Occupation) Convention (C 111). However, Article 12(2) of the Constitution provides, among other things, that there shall be no discrimination against citizens of Singapore on the ground only of religion, race, descent or place of birth in any appointment to any office or employment under public authority. Nonetheless, as is self-evident from the wording, this only applies to the actions of the State in appointing persons to public office. Thus, private employers are under no such legal obligation, and even in relation to the government, not all forms of discrimination are covered (such as discrimination based on gender, age or sexual orientation).

---

25. *See*, for instance, s. 2(1) of the Employment Act.
26. *See* s. 95A of the Employment Act.

38. Though there is no general anti-discrimination law in Singapore, there is a Tripartite Alliance for Fair Employment Practices which has introduced some guidelines. These guidelines call for non-discrimination in the hiring process, among other things. These guidelines have also been widely publicized in the media and even appear on billboards. Thus though they are not legally binding, they seemed to have had some effect. For instance, it has been reported that the number of discriminatory advertisements has decreased drastically since these guidelines have come out. It is likely that the reason why Singapore does not have general anti-discrimination legislation is the fear that the whole process may be cumbersome and could have significant cost implications on the employer. It should also be highlighted that though the guidelines are not legally enforceable, there can be indirect administrative sanctions for not complying, and such mechanisms also play an important part.

§3. Length of Contract

39. In terms of the length of the contract, there is no minimum or maximum length. As a matter of practice, it is common to have contracts of unspecified duration. However, some statutory provisions, especially under the Employment Act, confer certain rights depending on the length of employment. For instance, by virtue of section 76(2A) of the Employment Act, before a female employee can claim maternity leave against her employer, she has to have been employed for at least three months prior to the delivery with that employer. Since a contract does not have to be of a minimum length and some statutory rights depend on the length of service, it is possible for employers to have contracts of very short duration with gaps in between the old contract and the new contract to avoid statutory obligations, though such practices may not be that prevalent.

§4. Variation of Contract

40. Once a contract has been entered into, generally, the parties are not free to vary it. However, there are exceptions to this rule. These include the situation where the contract clearly and expressly provides for the variation in question, the situation where the variation is by way of seal or deed, the situation where both parties agree and obtain some fresh benefit as a result of the variation, the situation where one party varies the contract without fraud or dishonesty on his part, and the other agrees and obtains an indirect benefit or avoids a detriment[27] and the situation where the doctrine of promissory estoppel applies.[28] Typically, most employment contracts will have a standard clause allowing the employer to make variations. It is also common for contracts to provide that the salary payable is subject to a monthly variable component so that the employer retains the flexibility to deal with sudden unfavourable economic conditions.

27. *See*, for instance, *Sea-Land Service Inc. v. Cheong Fook Chee Vincent* [1994] 3 SLR (R) 250.
28. *Ibid.*

§5. Probation

41. Some contracts also provide for probation, though not all. It is common for contracts to provide different rights to employees on probation, especially in relation to the amount of notice to be given to terminate the contract before confirmation. However, in terms of statutory rights, generally, the probationary employee will be entitled to all the rights as a confirmed employee would be. Nonetheless, if a confirmed employee does not qualify for a statutory right (for instance, as would not a female employee who has worked for fewer than ninety days before delivery, seeking maternity leave against her employer) then, the probationary employee would not either.

§6. Factors Affecting Contracts

42. Even if a contract has been entered into, in some situations, it may not be enforceable. The two most common situations are minority and illegality.

I. Minors

43. Under section 12(2) of the Employment Act, a contract with a person less than 18 years of age cannot be enforced against that person unless the contract is for his benefit. This is to protect minors, but no civil cases have arisen in Singapore in this connection. This is probably so because most modern employment contracts will be beneficial as the minor will be learning something, earning something and will be able to resign if he does not like the job.

44. Aside from the civil aspect, reference must also be made to the criminal aspect. Pursuant to the Employment (Children and Young Persons) Regulations, it is a criminal offence to hire someone who is less than 13 years of age. Someone who is more than 13, but less than 15, can be employed in non-industrial undertakings subject to some restrictions such as that he cannot be employed as a workman[29] for more than six hours in a day. However, such a person generally cannot be hired in an industrial undertaking in view of the risks involved. In contrast, a person who is more than 15, but less than 16, can even be hired in industrial undertakings, but again subject to certain restrictions such as that he cannot be employed as a workman for more than seven hours in a day. There is a definition of what amounts to an industrial undertaking in the Employment Act, and breach of these provisions results in the commission of offence on the part of the employer and the parent or guardian who knowingly or negligently permits such employment.[30] However, there have been no criminal prosecutions in this area as a matter of practice as the illegal employment of children, or young persons is not common in Singapore.

---

29. As to 'workman', *see* para. 14.
30. Section 74 of the Employment Act.

45. It must also be highlighted that Singapore has ratified the International Labour Organization's Minimum Age Convention (No. 138) and Worst Forms of Child Labour Convention (No. 182).

II. Illegality and Foreign Workers

46. As mentioned above, another situation in which a contract entered into may not be enforceable is if it is illegal. This can especially arise in the context of foreign workers who are hired without proper work passes or permits. In Singapore, subject to a few exceptions (such as foreign students of certain educational organizations working during school holidays),[31] any employer wishing to employ someone who is not a citizen or permanent resident of Singapore has to apply for a 'work pass' that permits that person to work in Singapore. This is pursuant to the Employment of Foreign Manpower Act.[32] Failure to obtain a work pass is an offence on the part of both the employer and the employee.[33]

47. There are several kinds of work pass, the most common being the work permit, the 'S pass' and the employment pass. All passes are issued by the Controller of Work Passes at the Ministry of Manpower and are typically subject to conditions. These conditions may be imposed on the employer and on the employee. For instance, in relation to an employee who is hired on a work permit, the conditions would provide that the employee should only work for the employer named in the pass and not for some other employer. Breach of the conditions also results in the commission of an offence.[34]

48. The work permit is the lowest category and applies to unskilled workers, such as construction workers and cleaners. To discourage over-reliance on foreign workers, the employer must pay a monthly levy to the government in respect of each foreign worker he hires on a work permit and must employ a certain number of local workers before he can hire an additional foreign worker on a work permit. In addition, the employer must furnish a security bond in respect of all employees who are hired on work permits (with the exception of Malaysian nationals) to ensure that it is the employer (and not, for example, the government) that is financially responsible for matters such as the worker's eventual repatriation.

49. The S pass is the middle category of work pass and covers 'semi-skilled' workers, such as technicians and nurses. As with work permits, the employer must pay a monthly levy to the government in respect of each foreign worker it hires on an S pass and must employ a certain number of local workers before it can hire an additional foreign worker on an S pass. However, the employer does not have to

31. *See* Employment of Foreign Manpower (Work Pass Exemptions) Notification (S 345/2007).
32. Section 5 of the Employment of Foreign Manpower Act.
33. *Ibid.*
34. Section 22 of the Employment of Foreign Manpower Act.

provide a security bond in relation to workers hired on an S pass, the rationale being that S pass holders are likely to have the financial means to meet eventualities such as repatriation.

50. The employment pass is the highest category of work pass and covers skilled workers such as professionals. To encourage the employment of highly skilled foreigners in Singapore, the employer is not subject to levies, quota restrictions or security bonds in relation to the hiring of employees on employment passes.

51. Generally, foreign workers are entitled to the same statutory rights as local workers, with the exception of some foreign workers in some situations (such as domestic workers for the purposes of work injury compensation).[35] Also, as mentioned earlier,[36] Singapore has a very high percentage of foreign workers, but the percentage of workers who work illegally is small, given the tough enforcement measures.

---

35. *See* para. 15.
36. *See* para. 2.

Chapter 3. Duties of the Parties

§1. Duties of the Employee

52. The employee has various duties in a contract of employment. Some duties could arise because of an express requirement in the contract, some could arise as a result of implied terms, and some could arise as a result of statutes.

I. Express Duties

53. In relation to duties that emanate via express terms, since much depends on what the express term in question provides, nothing more will be said of them; examples could be a clause in the contract of employment which prohibits any form of outside work without the employer's consent or a clause which places some restriction on the use of the Internet or social media or a clause which prohibits the disclosure of confidential information. Generally, as mentioned earlier,[37] subject to a few exceptions, such as non-compete clauses[38] or liquidated damages clauses, express terms are valid and cannot be challenged.

II. Implied Duties

54. In addition to express terms, a contract may also have implied terms.[39] While the various commonly implied terms are discussed below, it must be highlighted that it is possible for the contract to have an express clause governing the very same issues. It is also possible for such clauses to place an even more onerous duty on the employee. Also, as previously mentioned,[40] it is not possible for an implied term to override an express term.

A. Duty of Obedience

55. One implied duty on the part of the employee is to be obedient and to follow the instructions of the employer[41] as the employment relationship naturally envisages one person issuing instructions and the other person following them. However, if the instructions are unreasonable, unlawful or involve some additional risks over and above what the employee expressly or impliedly agreed to do, then the

37. *See* para. 28.
38. *See* para. 212.
39. *See* para. 29.
40. *Ibid.*
41. *See*, for instance, *Lim Chuan Cheng v. The Borneo Co Ltd* (1964) 30 MLJ 351.

employee is not obliged to obey such an instruction.[42] Depending on the circumstances,[43] disobedience that is unjustified in the circumstances may entitle the employer to terminate the services of the employee on the spot without notice or salary in lieu of notice. For instance, in *Nappalli Peter Williams v. ITE*,[44] where a school teacher refused to follow the school's policy of participation in the pledge and national anthem ceremony because of his religious beliefs, it was held that he was rightly dismissed summarily.

B. Duty to Take Reasonable Care

56. Another implied duty on the part of the employee is to perform his task with reasonable care and skill.[45] The amount of care and skill the employee is expected to have would vary with the circumstances. For instance, if an employee is a professional and holds himself out as having certain skills, then the expectation would be higher than for an unskilled person. Again depending on the circumstances,[46] a breach of this duty may allow the employer to terminate the services of the employee on the spot without notice or salary in lieu of notice. He may also be able to sue for damages.

C. Duty of Good Faith

57. Yet another implied term on the part of the employee is that he has a duty of good faith towards the employer. This is a very general duty and can encompass many matters.

58. For instance, the employee should not misappropriate the property of the employer.[47] In this context, the property can also include documents. The duty of good faith would also mean that the employee should give due consideration to the interests of the employer. For instance, an employee should not place himself in a position where his duty and interests conflict[48] and should not take a bribe or make a secret profit. However, the exact limits of this duty depend on the type of employee in question. If the employee is a fiduciary who is placed in a position of trust (such as a director), he will owe greater duties.[49]

59. The duty of good faith can also have implications in relation to doing outside work. If the employer's interests are likely to be jeopardized if the employee

42. *See*, for instance, *Yong Yoke Sung v. Sungei Way Estate* [1966] 1 MLJ 175.
43. *See* para. 198 onwards.
44. [1999] 2 SLR (R) 569.
45. *See*, for instance, *Lee Siew Chun v. Sourgrapes Packaging Products Trading Pte Ltd* [1992] 3 SLR (R) 858.
46. *See* para. 198 onwards.
47. *See*, for instance, *Motilal v. Gutherie Agency (M) Ltd* [1968] 1 MLJ 211.
48. *See*, for instance, *Viking Airtech Pte Ltd v. Foo Teow Keng* [2008] 1 SLR (R) 225.
49. *See*, for instance, *Nagase Singapore Pte Ltd v. Ching Kai Huat* [2007] 3 SLR (R) 265.

does such outside work (for instance, the employee is in a position to pass confidential information to a competitor and seeks to work for a competitor), then the employee will be under an implied duty not to do such outside work.[50]

60. Preparing to compete or work for a competitor may also result in the breach of the duty of good faith depending on various factors. For instance, just attending an interview with a competitor would not amount to a breach. On the other hand, actively soliciting clients or entering into contracts with suppliers or recruiting staff for a competing business may amount to a breach. For instance, *in Abdul Latif Bin Mohammed Tahiar v. Saeed Husain s/o Hakin Gulam Mohiudi*,[51] the employer was in the business of hiring out chauffeur-driven cars. The employee in question, while working for the employer, secretly registered a competing business and managed to get two contracts from existing clients of the employer. The court held that the employee had breached the duty of good faith and was liable for the losses suffered by the employer.

61. The duty of good faith also means that the employee has a duty to observe confidentiality. This duty applies not only during the contract of employment but even after the contract of employment has come to an end, though in relation to the latter situation, only information that is highly confidential or which can amount to a trade secret is likely to be protected.[52] Whether information is highly confidential will depend on various factors such as the position of the employee, whether the information is available to the public, whether disclosure of the information can be reasonably injurious to the employer or advantageous to his rival.[53]

62. Depending on the circumstances,[54] a breach of the duty of good faith may entitle the employer to terminate the services of the employee on the spot without notice or salary in lieu of notice. He may also be able to sue for damages. It may also be possible to obtain an injunction to stop the employee or ex-employee from doing certain things, such as disclosing confidential information.

D. Making Disclosures

63. While the employee has various duties, as discussed above, he does not have a duty to make disclosures about himself or others as this would impose an unreasonably onerous duty on the employee. Nonetheless, there are exceptions to this rule. For instance, if the employee is specifically asked a question, he cannot give a false answer. Similarly, if the employee is a fiduciary, he may have a duty to disclose, for instance, his misdeeds. Thus in *Goh Kim Hai Edward v. Pacific Can*

50. *See*, for instance, *Pacific Autocom Enterprise Pte Ltd v. Chia Wah Siang* [2004] 3 SLR(R) 73.
51. [2003] 2 SLR (R) 61.
52. *Tang Siew Choy v. Certact Pte Ltd* [1993] 1 SLR (R) 835.
53. *Ibid.*
54. *See* para. 198 onwards.

Investment Holdings Ltd,[55] it was held that when the board of directors was proceeding to consider the renewal of his contract, the director in question, being a fiduciary, should have disclosed all facts that might have affected their deliberations. Likewise, if the employee has supervisory functions, he may have a duty to disclose the misdeeds of others in the organization.

E. Intellectual Property

64. It should also be highlighted that in the absence of an express agreement to the contrary, an employee does not have the right to inventions and works made in the course of his work; that is, the intellectual property rights in these works and inventions vest with the employer and not the employee unless the contract provides otherwise. As a matter of practice, it is not common for the contract to provide otherwise.

This general principle is also reflected in various statutes such as the Copyright Act,[56] the Patents Act and the Registered Designs Act.

III. Statutory Duties

65. Aside from duties arising from the contract, the employee may also have some duties which emanate from the statute. For instance, pursuant to section 15 of the Workplace Safety and Health Act, if the employee is careless in terms of health and safety at the workplace or fails to use the protective equipment provided, he could face criminal liabilities under that Act.

§2. Duties of the Employer

66. Just like the employee, the employer may have various duties, and these may emanate from the express terms of the contract or may be implied or may arise as a result of a statutory provision.

I. Express Duties

67. In relation to express terms, since much would depend on the exact wording of the express term in question, nothing more would be said about them, but an example could be an express term guaranteeing a certain amount of bonus or an express term guaranteeing certain insurance payouts in the event of certain eventualities.

55. [1996] 1 SLR (R) 540.
56. *See also The Performing Right Society Ltd v. United Artists Singapore Theatres Pte Ltd* [2001] 1 SLR (R) 488.

II. Implied Duties

68. In relation to implied terms, the employer is subject to numerous implied duties, and these are considered below.

A. *Duty to Take Reasonable Care*

69. One of the implied terms relating to the employer is the duty of care he owes towards his employee, and this is an often litigated area. The duty of care is a general duty[57] and can mean many things. For instance, the employer must have competent staff, and if the employer does not have competent staff and, as a result, another employee is injured, the employer could end up being liable. Likewise, if an employee sexually harasses or bullies another employee and the employer knows or ought to know and does not address the situation when he could reasonably have done so, that may also amount to a breach of the duty of care. This duty would also mean that the employer must have a safe system of working and provide safe equipment. He may also have to provide adequate safety equipment and give adequate instructions and carry out adequate supervision. As established in *Chandran a/l Subbiah v. Dockers Marine Pte Ltd*,[58] this duty may also encompass making risk assessments before dispatching an employee to an external place of work. Further, as part of this duty, the employer could even be liable for psychiatric harm caused to the employee, which could, for instance, have arisen due to work-related stress, though there have been no local cases on this point. While the employer owes a wide duty, as discussed above, whether the employer is actually in breach of that duty depends on whether the employer failed to do what another reasonable employer would have done in the circumstances.[59] However, even if there is a breach of duty, the employer who is sued may have some defences. One of the main defences is contributory negligence on the part of the employee.[60] If this is established, the amount of damages to be awarded to the employee may be reduced. However, by virtue of section 2(1) of the Unfair Contract Terms Act, it is not possible for the employer to exclude liability for negligence that results in personal injury or death. In addition, as established in *Wee Peng Whatt v. Singapore Transport Supply Services Pte Ltd*,[61] delegation of duty is not a defence, the idea being that otherwise, it would be easy for employers to escape liability.

B. *Duty to Indemnify*

70. Another implied duty on the part of the employer is to indemnify the employee in respect of any expenses, losses or liabilities, which he may reasonably

57. *Chandran a/l Suppiah v. Dockers Marine Pte Ltd* [2010] 1 SLR 786.
58. [2010] 1 SLR 786.
59. *Chandran a/l Suppiah v. Dockers Marine Pte Ltd* [2010] 1 SLR 786.
60. *See*, for instance, *Parno v. SC Marine Pte Ltd* [1999] 3 SLR (R) 377.
61. [1977–1978] SLR (R) 229.

incur in the discharge of his duties.[62] However, the duty to indemnify may be circumscribed by express terms of the contract. For instance, the contract could provide that if the employee is seeking a reimbursement for a travel expense, this has to be done within a certain time frame, failing which no reimbursement will be provided. In addition, there is no duty to indemnify the employee where the expenses are incurred as a result of the employee's negligence or wrongdoing unless the contract expressly provides otherwise.

C. Duty to Protect Confidential Information

71. Yet another implied duty on the part of the employer is not to disclose confidential information pertaining to the employee to others who are not authorized to receive the information. However, there could be some defences, such as that the disclosure was made in the public interest. There are yet to be any local cases on this issue.

D. Duty to Treat Employees with Trust and Confidence

72. Another very important implied duty is that the employer must treat the employee with trust and confidence.[63] This can encompass many things. For instance, this duty could be breached if the employer uses abusive language, fails to inquire into complaints relating to matters such as sexual harassment or health and safety issues at work, forces the employee to go for medical examinations when there is no reasonable need to do so or unilaterally varies the contract of employment to the detriment of the employee. It is also possible that this duty extends to according the employee sufficient privacy at work, but the exact ambits of this have not been clearly established, and thus typically, employers may have express terms covering such matters such as conducting searches. Further, while the duty is quite wide, it would appear that it does not extend to the issue of termination of the contract of employment or dismissal, in that, the employer has no duty of trust or confidence in relation to such matters. However, there may be some limited statutory limitations which would be discussed later.[64] If the duty is breached depending on the circumstances,[65] the employee may resign on the spot without giving notice or salary in lieu of notice. He may also be able to sue for losses if any.

---

62. *See*, for instance, *Chaly Chee Keong Mah v. The Liquidators of Baring Futures (Singapore) Pte Ltd* [2003] 2 SLR (R) 571.
63. *Chan Miu Yin v. Philip Morris Singapore Pte Ltd* [2011] SGHC 161. The cases that have recognized this term thus far have all been High Court decisions. However, the recent Court of Appeal decision, *Wee Kim San Lawrence Bernard v. Robinson & Co (Singapore) Pte Ltd* [2014] SGCA 43, has left open the question of whether there was indeed such an implied term in Singapore.
64. *See* para. 189 onwards.
65. *See* para. 198 onwards.

E. Generally No Duty to Provide Work

73. While the employer owes various implied duties, the employer is unlikely to owe an implied duty to provide a certain amount of work.[66] In a contract of employment, the usual duty of the employer is to provide remuneration rather than to provide work. However, there are exceptions. For instance, if the employee is remunerated by the commission, there might be an expectation that the employer would be promising a reasonable amount of work that would earn those commissions. Nonetheless, even in relation to the exceptions, it is possible to have an express clause in the contract to state that the employer is not promising any work in such circumstances.

III. Statutory Duties

74. Aside from express or implied terms, the employer may also incur other obligations by virtue of some statutory provision. But before examining the statutory obligations, some obligations that are *not* statutorily provided for in Singapore would first be highlighted.

A. Minimum Wage

75. Singapore does not have any legislation on a minimum wage. Singapore has also not ratified the International Labour Organization's Minimum Wage Fixing Convention (No. 131). However, in recent times, there have been some calls for the introduction of minimum wages. Singapore's main reservation about introducing minimum wages appears to be that it could create inflexibility, which could have an adverse effect on businesses.

76. Nonetheless, Singapore does try to address the problems faced by low wage workers in various ways. To begin with, there is subsidized health care, education and public housing. In addition, there is a workfare income supplement scheme implemented by the government to support low wage workers who are Singapore citizens. In this way, the cost is borne by the government and not businesses. Many other new initiatives are also continuously explored. For instance, certain industries (namely, cleaning, security services and landscaping) need to pay their workers a minimum salary in order to keep their business licences. This is a more targeted approach in that the minimum salary can vary from industry to industry and it is not fixed but progressive depending on skills. Though these initiatives do not apply to foreign employees, there are plans to bring more local employees working in different sectors such as escalator maintenance, waste management and retail, within this framework

66. *See*, for instance, *K.V. Pillai v. Power Foam Rubber Products (MFG) Co Ltd* (1963) MLJ 268.

B. Retrenchment Benefits

77. Another area in which there is no legislation in favour of the employee relates to the payment of retrenchment benefits. The reason for the lack of such legislation is probably the fact that if the employer is not in the best of financial health, making him pay a certain fixed amount to each of his employees may make the business even more susceptible to failure. In fact, under section 45 of the Employment Act, it is provided that for employees falling under the Employment Act,[67] the contract or collective agreement cannot provide for retrenchment benefits for workers who have worked for less than three years with the employer in question. This is because new businesses which have just been set up generally need more time to grow and become financially stable before they can bear the burden of making such payments.

78. Subject to section 45 of the Employment Act, as a matter of practice, retrenchment benefits are quite commonly provided for in collective agreements. They are also quite commonly paid out of discretion or goodwill.

C. Discrimination

79. Yet another area in which Singapore does not have any laws is in relation to discrimination. As mentioned earlier,[68] the Constitution refers to non-discrimination, but this only applies to certain types of discrimination and applies only to government appointments. Further, the Constitution does not deal with discrimination during the job or discrimination relating to the termination of the job. Singapore has also not ratified the International Labour Organization's Discrimination (Employment and Occupation) Convention (No. 111). However, Singapore has ratified the United Nations Convention on the Elimination of All Forms of Discrimination against Women (1979). Even then, there is no local legislation that incorporates all the principles enunciated therein into practice.

80. Though there is no local legislation, there is a Tripartite Alliance on Fair Employment Practices which provides guidelines pertaining to non-discrimination. For instance, these guidelines provide for what can be stated in job advertisements and job applications and on what can be asked during job interviews. The guidelines also emphasize that remuneration should be on the basis of performance, contribution and experience of the employee and that they should not be on the basis of age, gender, race or religion of the employee. These guidelines appear to have had some effect. Though they are not legally enforceable and there can be some indirect administrative sanctions for a breach. However, the guidelines themselves are a little vague and do not cover many things such as discrimination on the basis of country of origin. For instance, in relation to low wage workers, it is common for Singaporean workers to be paid more than their counterparts from foreign countries

67. *See* para. 10.
68. *See* para. 37.

who come to work in Singapore for doing the same job, the justification of employers being that foreign workers chose to come here to work at those rates whereas local workers would not want to do those jobs unless they are paid more.

D. Equal Remuneration

81. Another area in which Singapore does not have any legislation is in relation to equal remuneration. Singapore has ratified the International Labour Organization's Equal Remuneration Convention (No. 100), which calls for equal pay for work of equal value regardless of gender. However, there is no local legislation that puts this into practice, though, as mentioned earlier, there is a Tripartite Alliance for Fair Employment Practices, which promotes the adoption of such equal treatment. In addition, some collective agreements have provisions requiring the employer to observe equality.

E. Other Areas Not Covered by Statute

82. It may also be pointed out that Singapore also does not have any statutory provisions relating to certain forms of leave, such as study leave or compassionate leave.

83. There is also no statutory duty to pay various types of allowances such as food allowances or housing allowances though, in relation to lower-level foreign employees hired under work permits,[69] the employer may have a statutory obligation to provide food and accommodation pursuant to the work permit conditions breach of which results in the commission of an offence.[70]

84. Singapore also does not have any specific statutory laws on sexual harassment at the workplace. It is also not mandatory for businesses to have any internal code on sexual harassment in place. However, the recently passed Prevention of Harassment Act provides some remedies (including seeking protection orders and claiming damages) in respect of harassment, regardless of the context in which it takes place.

85. Further, Singapore does not have the concept of unemployment benefits though the government does have in place some temporary assistance schemes to help the less fortunate (who may or may not be employed). Non-governmental organizations also provide for various forms of assistance. In addition, the government does have various schemes (such as the provision of subsidized courses) for the upgrading of skills which will make the unemployed more employable.

---

69. *See* para. 47.
70. Section 22 of the Employment of Foreign Manpower Act.

86. In terms of taxation, Singapore also does not have the pay-as-you-earn system, which obliges the employer to make deductions for tax at source. However, in relation to foreign employees, there are some obligations on the employer to withhold tax in certain circumstances under the Income Tax Act.[71]

F. Areas Covered by Statute

87. Having looked at the statutory provisions Singapore does not have, reference will now be made to statutory provisions Singapore does have. Other than the Workplace Safety and Health Act, the Personal Data Protection Act and the Retirement and Re-employment Act, the other statutes will be covered in other parts of this work, and hence reference will only be made to these three statutes at this juncture.

G. Workplace Safety and Health Act

88. Formally workplace safety was governed by the Factories Act, but it was much narrower in terms of coverage of premises and persons who owed duties. In contrast, by virtue of section 2 of the Workplace Safety and Health Act, all premises are covered, except for a few, such as domestic premises.

89. Under section 12(1) of the Workplace Safety and Health Act, the employer is obliged to take reasonably practicable measures that are necessary to ensure the safety and health of his employees. The subsections of section 12 provide some general guidance as to what exactly this duty encompasses. For instance, they provide that the employer has to develop and implement procedures for dealing with emergencies and ensure that persons at work have adequate instructions, information, training and supervision. However, the subsections are not meant to be exhaustive, the idea being that employers have to be proactive in dealing with safety issues, and it would not be sufficient to merely follow a preset prescribed standard. Nonetheless, there are many regulations made under the Workplace Safety and Health Act, which deal with diverse matters ranging from construction to first aid, and these provide for detailed and specific duties as well. It should also be highlighted that under the Workplace Safety and Health Act, there can be a liability if there is merely a risk, without there being an accident.[72] Breach of the provisions of the Workplace Health and Safety Act and/or the regulations made under that Act result in a commission of an offence by the employer.[73] There also appears to be no well-established defence for a breach on the part of the employer. Under the Workplace Safety and Health Act, the employer may also be issued with a stop order or a remedial order in the interest of safety, a breach of which is also an offence.[74]

71. Section 68 of the Income Tax Act.
72. *See*, for instance, s. 11 of the Workplace Safety and Health Act.
73. *See*, for instance, s. 50 of the Workplace Safety and Health Act.
74. Section 21 of the Workplace Safety and Health Act.

90. In addition, under the Workplace Safety and Health Act, besides employers, many others owe duties. These include occupiers,[75] principals,[76] self-employed persons,[77] persons at work[78] and even manufacturers and suppliers of certain machinery and equipment.[79] It is also possible for more than one person to be liable in any given circumstance, as provided in section 10.

91. While the Workplace Safety and Health Act is generally all-encompassing and the penalties for breaches are hefty (up to SGD 1 million for repeat corporate offenders),[80] the statute itself does not give rise to civil liability. The employee who is injured would have to sue for a breach of duty of care[81] instead or claim under the Work Injury Compensation Act.[82]

H. Personal Data Protection Act

92. As mentioned, another statute that imposes an obligation on the employer is the recently enacted Personal Data Protection Act. Under section 3 of the Personal Data Protection Act, all organizations are covered. However, section 4 provides for some exceptions, such as in the case of public agencies. Thus, employees of public agencies will not receive any protection under the Personal Data Protection Act, though public agencies are likely to have internal rules governing such matters.

93. The broad aim of the Personal Data Protection Act is set out in section 3, and it is to govern the collection, use and disclosure of personal data by organizations in a manner that recognizes both the right of the individuals to protect their personal data and the need of organizations to collect, use and disclose personal data for purposes that a reasonable person would consider appropriate in the circumstances. Under section 13 of the Personal Data Protection Act, an organization is not to collect, use or disclose personal data about an individual unless the individual gives or is deemed to give his consent or some statutory exception applies.

94. In this regard, there are many statutory exceptions relating to the employment situation set out in the Schedules to the Personal Data Protection Act. One exception relates to the situation where personal data are necessary for investigation or proceedings.[83] Another exception relates to a situation where personal data are necessary for evaluative purposes, for instance, in the hiring, managing or terminating of the employment relationship.[84]

---

75. Section 11 of the Workplace Safety and Health Act.
76. Section 14 of the Workplace Safety and Health Act.
77. Section 13 of the Workplace Safety and Health Act.
78. Section 15 of the Workplace Safety and Health Act.
79. Section 16 of the Workplace Safety and Health Act.
80. Section 51 of the Workplace Safety and Health Act.
81. *See* para. 69.
82. *See* para. 155.
83. *See*, for instance, para. 1(e) of the Second Schedule to the Personal Data Protection Act.
84. *See*, for instance, para. 1(f) of the Second Schedule to the Personal Data Protection Act.

95. Under section 21 of the Personal Data Protection Act, the individual is also given the right to access personal data. However, again in the employment context, there is a major exception, namely, opinion data kept solely for evaluative purposes as provided for in the Fifth Schedule to the Act. Thus, for instance, an employee cannot request to see opinion data about him contained in an annual review form.

96. Under the Personal Data Protection Act, organizations are also requested to take reasonable security measures to protect personal data[85] and are obliged not to retain personal data for longer than necessary.[86]

97. There are limited criminal liabilities under the Personal Data Protection Act for things such as the fraudulent alteration of personal data in records.[87] Otherwise, the main consequence for a breach is the possibility of the imposition of a financial penalty (up to SGD 1 million)[88] on the employer, though it is likely that as a matter of practice, such huge penalties would not be imposed other than in the most blatant of breaches. Further, by virtue of section 53 of the Personal Data Protection Act, employers are liable for the actions of employees acting in the course of employment, but employees themselves are generally not liable under the Personal Data Protection Act for such breaches. Aside from all this, an employee who suffers loss or damage directly as a result of a contravention of some part of the Personal Data Protection Act may also be able to bring a civil action pursuant to section 32 of that Act.

I. Retirement and Re-employment Act

98. Another statute that imposes obligations on the employer is the Retirement and Re-employment Act. Pursuant to section 7 and 7A of the Retirement and Re-employment Act, when an employee reaches the age of 62 or any higher retirement age as provided in the contract. The retirement age will go up to 63 in 2022 and 65 by 2030. After reaching the retirement age, the employer has to offer the employee re-employment up until the age of 67, provided the employee's work performance has been satisfactory, and he or she is medically fit to continue. The period of re-employment will be extended to the age of 70 by 2030. Such a system of retirement and re-employment gives the employer some flexibility.

99. If these criteria are met, the employer has to offer re-employment unless it can establish that there is no suitable vacancy in its organization, despite making reasonable attempts to find one.[89] If the employer establishes that there is no such vacancy, generally, the employer has to compensate the employee as provided for

85. Section 24 of the Personal Data Protection Act.
86. Section 25 of the Personal Data Protection Act.
87. Section 51 of the Personal Data Protection Act.
88. Section 29 of the Personal Data Protection Act.
89. Section 7C of the Retirement and Re-employment Act.

in section 7C of the Retirement and Re-employment Act. However, the amount of compensation is determined by tripartite guidelines and is currently modest.

100. Even if the employer does offer re-employment, it can be on different terms than the employee's previous employment as provided for in section 7A of the Retirement and Re-employment Act, though any variation has to be based on reasonable factors. The employee is also not obliged to accept the offer of re-employment as set out in section 7A.

101. There are statutory mechanisms in place to resolve disputes relating to re-employment, such as whether the employee's work performance was satisfactory or whether the employer did not have any suitable vacancy.[90] These statutory mechanisms include mediation and appeal to the Minister of Manpower. It would have been simpler to merely raise the retirement age, but the idea behind the Retirement and Re-employment Act is to offer the employer more flexibility.

90. *See* ss 8A–8C of the Retirement and Re-employment Act.

Chapter 4. Working Time and Leave

§1. Working Time

102. The Employment Act has provisions concerning working hours. However, as mentioned earlier,[91] the Employment Act does not apply to all employees. In addition, the provisions relating to working hours fall under Part IV of the Employment Act. Part IV of the Employment Act only applies to employees earning SGD 2,600 or less a month or who are workmen,[92] in which case their salary must be SGD 4,500 or less a month.

103. Assuming the employee falls under Part IV of the Employment Act, the relevant section dealing with working hours is section 38. Section 38(1)b provides that no employee is required to work for more than eight hours a day or for more than forty-four hours a week. However, there are many exceptions. For instance, under section 38(1), if the employee works less than eight hours on any particular day, he may be required to work for more than eight hours on any other day, and if the employee works for not more than five days in a week (which is quite common), he may be required to work more than eight hours a day, though, in both situations, the employee cannot be required to work for more than nine hours a day or for more than forty-four hours a week. Similarly, for shift workers, section 40 allows the limits stated above to be exceeded, provided the average number of hours worked over a continuous period of three weeks does not exceed forty-four hours per week. That aside, in some other situations, as provided for in section 38(2), such as where urgent work needs to be done to machinery or plant, or where there has been an interruption of work which it was impossible to foresee or where there has been an accident, the limits set out in section 38(1) may be exceeded. Also, interestingly, under section 41A, it is possible for the employer to seek the permission of the Commissioner of Labour to exceed the limits, and the Commissioner may grant such permission after considering the operational needs of the employer and the health and safety of the employee or class of employees concerned. The idea of this provision is to provide flexibility, especially for companies that may face demands during some periods but not during others where there may not be much work and employees could afford to work less hours. This is another example of how labour law in Singapore seeks to balance the competing interests of the various parties.

104. Breach of the provisions of Part IV of the Employment Act results in a commission of an offence under section 53. For employees not falling under Part IV, there are no limits as to the working hours. However, the employer still owes the employee an implied duty of care,[93] and this might place some implied limitation on how much the employer can expect the employee to work, but there are no local cases on this point.

---

91. *See* para. 10.
92. *See* para. 14.
93. *See* para. 69.

§2. Overtime Work

105. Even in relation to the limits mentioned above, the employee is not barred from working beyond those limits. It is just that if he works beyond those limits, he would be entitled to overtime pay. In this regard, section 38(4) provides that the overtime pay should not be less than one and half times the employee's hourly basic rate of pay. However, for this to apply, the work must be at the request of the employer. Thus if the employer does not request the employee to remain to complete the work, the employee cannot claim overtime. It must also be mentioned that the employer cannot escape this duty to pay overtime by giving time-off in lieu. Nonetheless, there are exceptions to the rule requiring payment for overtime work. For instance, under section 41A referred to above, if a company goes through cycles and during particular months demand peaks and during other months demand falls, the employer, with the permission of the Commissioner, may ask the employee to work in excess of his required hours during the peak periods and not pay over time, but give him time-off during the lull periods.

106. It must also be mentioned that there is a limit to the amount of overtime work. The basic principle as set out in section 38 is that no employee can be required to work for more than twelve hours in a day or for more than seventy-two hours in a month. Nonetheless, again there are exceptions, such as section 41A referred to above.

107. Overtime pay appears in Part IV of the Employment Act.[94] As mentioned earlier, a breach of Part IV of the Employment Act results in a commission of an offence under section 53.

108. For employees not falling under Part IV, there is no obligation to pay overtime pay unless the contract or collective agreement provides otherwise, though this is not common as a matter of practice.

§3. Rest Days

109. As for rest days, these are set out in Part IV of the Employment Act as well,[95] a breach of which results in the commission of an offence under section 53. For employees not falling under Part IV of the Employment Act, whether the employee is entitled to a rest day depends on the contract of employment, though most employers usually do grant employees at least one day of rest in a week. Many grant two. Foreign domestic workers, who are not covered by the Employment Act, are entitled to one day of rest per week, though it is possible for the employer to give payment in lieu of rest days if both parties mutually agree. This is provided for by the Employment of Foreign Manpower (Work Pass) Regulations, a breach of which results in the commission of an offence.

---

94. *See* para. 102.
95. *Ibid.*

110. For employees falling under Part IV of the Employment Act,[96] section 36(1) provides that they shall be entitled to one whole day of rest in a week without pay, which day can be a Sunday or such other day as may be determined from time to time by the employer. If the employee works on the rest day, he is entitled to additional pay. The amount of additional pay depends on whether the employer requested the employee to work on the rest day or the employee wanted to work on the rest day. Further, he may be entitled to overtime pay should he work for more than the normal hours of work on the rest day. However, in relation to all this, again, the section 41A exception referred to above[97] applies, the basic idea being, as mentioned, to create flexibility. It is possible for the contract or collective agreement to provide for more days of rest, and in practice, many employees only work five days a week.

§4. Annual Leave

111. Employees falling under the Employment Act are entitled to Annual Leave. This is under 88A of the Employment Act, and this does not fall under Part IV, and hence all employees covered under the Employment Act are entitled to Annual Leave For foreign domestic workers who are not covered by the Employment Act, the conditions of work permit do not have any provisions on annual leave, and hence they are not entitled to annual leave unless the employer decides to grant them such leave. In so far as the employee is contractually entitled to annual leave, it is unlikely that he would be entitled to payment in lieu for leave not taken unless the contract also provides for this. Since the concept of freedom of contract applies, it is also possible for the contract to provide that leave not taken would be forfeited should the employee serve notice of termination.

112. Section 88A(1) of the Employment Act provides that an employee who has served his employer for not less than three months will be entitled to paid annual leave of seven days in respect of the first year of continuous service with the same employer and one additional day for every subsequent year with the same employer, but subject to a maximum of fourteen days of annual leave. Though it is possible for the contract or collective agreement to provide for more days of leave, it is not possible for the contract or collective agreement to provide for worse terms relating to annual leave than those guaranteed by the Employment Act, such as that any leave not taken would be forfeited should the employee serve notice of termination.

113. If the employee has not worked for three months, then he will not have a statutory right to annual leave. There is also no statutory right to take half a day of leave as opposed to a full day of leave under the Employment Act though as a matter of practice, some employers do grant such leave. Pursuant to section 88A(6), generally, the leave has to be taken not later than twelve months after the end of every twelve months of continuous service. Thus, in essence, the leave can be rolled

96. *Ibid.*
97. *See* para. 103.

forward for up to a year. If the leave is not taken, the employee is not entitled to compensation with the exception of the situation where the employer terminates the contract of the employee other than for misconduct.[98]

§5. Public Holiday Leave

114. Employees falling under the Employment Act[99] are also entitled to paid public holiday leave. This is under section 88, and this does not fall under Part IV; and hence all employees covered under the Employment Act are entitled to public holidays. Generally, if the employee works on a public holiday, the employer has to either give a substituted paid day off[100] in lieu or give him additional pay (roughly double) for working on a public holiday.[101] If a public holiday falls on a rest day, the next day following will be a paid holiday.[102] It is a common practice to grant a half-day off on the eve of certain major religious holidays, but this is not a statutory right. A breach of section 88 of the Employment Act results in the commission of an offence under section 112 of that Act.

115. For employees not covered under the Employment Act, under the Holidays Act, they are entitled to leave on public holidays as well, but the Holidays Act is silent on the question of payment.

§6. Sick Leave

116. Employees falling under the Employment Act[103] are also entitled to paid sick leave. This is under section 89, and this does not fall under Part IV, and hence all employees covered under the Employment Act are entitled to paid sick leave. Section 89(1) provides that if an employee has served an employer for not less than six months, he shall be entitled to fourteen days of sick leave if no hospitalization is required and sixty days if hospitalization is required in any year. The maximum of both types of leave combined in any year is sixty days. The term 'year' is likely to refer to any period of twelve months. If the employee has not worked for six months with the employer but has worked for three months, he is entitled to pro-rated leave under section 89(2).

117. Besides giving pay during the period of sick leave, the employer must also bear the cost of medical examination. This does not include matters such as medication, ward charges or the cost of medical procedures undertaken. Nonetheless, many contracts and collective agreement provide for co-payment in relation to such other expenses.

---

98. Section 43(7) of the Employment Act.
99. *See* para. 10.
100. Section 88(1) of the Employment Act.
101. Section 88(4) of the Employment Act.
102. Section 88(1) of the Employment Act.
103. *See* para. 10.

118. However, before an employee can claim sick leave, he must meet certain preconditions. First, he must be certified by a medical practitioner or medical officer to be sick, and next, he must inform or attempt to inform the employer within forty-eight hours. This is pursuant to section 89(4) of the Employment Act. The term 'medical officer' as defined in section 2(1) of the Employment Act includes a registered dentist.

119. For employees not covered by the Employment Act, these matters would have to be determined by looking at the contract of employment. In practice, it is common for contracts of employment to provide for similar benefits. Even if there is no express clause, depending on the circumstances, in view of the duty of care,[104] it is likely to be an implied term that the employee should be granted sick leave if he is unable to work due to sickness, though there may not be an automatic corresponding implied right to receive payment during such sickness.

§7. Maternity Leave

120. There are two statutes governing maternity leave in Singapore. One is the Employment Act, and the other is the Child Development Co-Savings Act. The benefits under both these statutes are not identical. It is possible for some employees to fall under one but not the other. It is also possible for some employees to qualify under both statutes, in which case they would make use of the more beneficial of the two. Further, it is possible that an employee does not qualify under either of the statutes, in which case, her rights would depend on the contract of employment, though the implied duty of care[105] would suggest that the employee should be entitled to a reasonable period of rest after delivery. As for the Employment Act, as already mentioned,[106] it does not apply to all employees. However, the rights relating to maternity leave do not fall under Part IV of the Employment Act, and hence all employees covered by the Employment Act are entitled to maternity leave if they meet the prescribed conditions pertaining to maternity leave. As for the Child Development Co-Savings Act, all employees are covered, but there are also conditions pertaining to maternity leave and not all employees may meet those conditions.

I. Extent of Maternity Leave

121. Pursuant to section 76(1) of the Employment Act, essentially, there are three options in relation to maternity leave:

> period of four weeks immediately before and a period of eight weeks immediately after confinement;

104. *See* para. 69.
105. *Ibid.*
106. *See* para. 10.

a period of twelve weeks, as agreed to by the employee and her employer, commencing not earlier than twenty-eight days immediately preceding the day of confinement or later than that day; or

a period of eight weeks, as agreed to by the employee and her employer, commencing not earlier than twenty-eight days immediately preceding the day of confinement or later than that day, and to one or more further periods, not exceeding twenty-four days in aggregate, as agreed to by the employee and her employer, which shall be taken within twelve months commencing the day of her confinement.

122. Pursuant to section 9(1) of the Child Development Co-Savings Act, essentially, there are also three options in relation to maternity leave:

a period of four weeks immediately before and a period of twelve weeks immediately after confinement;

a period of sixteen weeks, as agreed to by the employee and her employer, commencing not earlier than twenty-eight days immediately preceding the day of confinement or later than that day; or

a period of eight weeks, as agreed to by the employee and her employer, commencing not earlier than twenty-eight days immediately preceding the day of confinement or later than that day, and to one or more further periods, not exceeding forty-eight days in aggregate, as agreed to by the employee and her employer, which shall be taken within twelve months commencing the day of her confinement.

123. As provided in section 2(1) of both statutes, the term 'confinement' refers to the delivery of a child. The third option under either statute provides the most flexibility and allows the female employee to take the maternity leave over a period of twelve months so that she can spend time with the child over a longer period. As for the third option, if the maternity leave is spread out, the exact number of days of entitlement depends on the number of days she normally works in a week. For instance, if an employee works five days a week, her entitlement under the Employment Act would be twenty days, and under the Child Co-Development Savings Act, it would be forty days. If she works five and a half days a week or more, her entitlement would be twenty-four days under the Employment Act and forty-eight days under the Child Development Co-Savings Act. However, as provided in section 76(6) of the Employment Act and section 9(3) of the Child Development Co-Savings Act, the drawback of the third option is that if the employment is terminated by either party for whatever reason, the balance of leave would be forfeited.

124. As can be seen, the benefits under the Child Co-Development Savings Act are more substantial. The Child Development Co-Savings Act was enacted subsequent to the enactment of the Employment Act in order to encourage more births but of Singapore citizens.

II. Preconditions for Maternity Leave

125. There are preconditions to be met under both statutes. One precondition as provided in section 76(2A) of the Employment Act and section 9A(1) of the Child Development Co-Savings Act is the requirement that the employee must have served at least three months prior to her confinement. Though this precondition is the same under either statute, under the Employment Act, there is no requirement that the child must be a Singapore citizen at the time of his birth. On the other hand, under section 9A(A) of the Child Development Co-Savings Act, there is such a requirement, though an exception applies when the child becomes a citizen within twelve months of birth.[107] As a result of this requirement, it is possible that some employees, such as foreigners working in Singapore, may not qualify under the Child Development Co-Savings Act. Another precondition that differs relates to the number of existing children. Under section 76(4) of the Employment Act, the employee is generally not entitled to maternity leave if she has two or more living children born during different confinements. On the other hand, under the Child Development Co-Savings Act, there is no limit as to the number of children.

III. Payment During Maternity Leave

126. There are also differences in relation to payment. Assuming the preconditions stated above are met, under the Employment Act, the employer is only obliged to pay for the first eight weeks as provided in section 76(1A), though the period of maternity leave is for twelve weeks in total. The amount of payment is not subject to any monetary limit. Thus, for instance, if the employee is earning SGD 20,000 every four weeks, the employer has to pay that amount for every four weeks of absence.

127. Under Child Development Co-Savings Act, assuming the preconditions stated above are met, there is a distinction between the first two confinements and subsequent ones. In respect of the first two confinements, as provided in section 9A(4) of the Child Development Co-Savings Act, the employer has to pay for the first eight weeks. This is not subject to any monetary limit. However, for the balance of the remaining eight weeks, the amount the employer has to pay is subject to a monetary limit of SGD 10,000 for a period of every four weeks. In relation to this payment, the employer can get a reimbursement from the government pursuant to section 10 of the Child Development Co-Savings Act. For children born outside the first two confinements, under section 9A(4) of the Child Development Co-Savings Act, the amount the employer is obliged to pay is subject to a limit of SGD 10,000 for a period of every four weeks, though again the employer can get a reimbursement for this from the government.

107. Section 9 of the Child Development Co-Savings Act.

128. Any employee who fails to make payment as stated above is guilty of an offence under section 87 of the Employment Act, and section 17(1) of the Child Development Co-Savings Act as the case may be.

IV. Avoiding Granting Maternity Leave

129. Where there is a statutory right to receive maternity leave, but the contract purports to deprive the employee of that right, the contractual provision would be null and void pursuant to section 86 of the Employment Act and section 12(1) of the Child Development Co-Savings Act. However, while there is maternity leave as described above, it must be highlighted that currently, there is no statutory provision allowing for taking time off in relation to antenatal care. Also, as stated earlier,[108] since there are no general anti-discrimination laws, there are no provisions relating to the non-hiring of pregnant women. Nonetheless, the Tripartite Alliance on Fair Employment Practices seeks to reduce the instances of such discrimination, though as said, these guidelines are non-binding.

§8. Paternity Leave

130. A female employee qualifies for maternity leave under the Child Development Co-Savings Act;[109] her husband may claim four weeks of her entitlement instead. There is no qualifying period for this option to be applicable. The employer (of the husband) who pays can get reimbursement from the government though this is subject to a limit of SGD 2,500 per week.

131. In addition, under the Child Development Co-Savings Act, if the father is lawfully married to the mother of the child and the child is a Singapore citizen, then the father would be entitled to up to two weeks of paternity leave. The leave can either be taken in one block or can be spread out over twelve months after the birth of the child. The employer who pays can get reimbursement from the government subject to a limit of SGD 2,500 per week. However, there is a qualifying period before the husband can claim paternity leave which is three months. The husband can take both forms of paternity-related leave.

§9. Childcare Leave

132. Just as with maternity leave, there are two statutes governing paid childcare leave. One is the Employment Act, and the other is the Child Development Co-Savings Act. The benefits under both these statutes are not identical. It is possible for some employees to fall under one but not the other. It is also possible for some employees to qualify under both statutes, in which case, they would make use

---

108. *See* para. 79.
109. *See* para. 125.

of the more beneficial of the two. In fact, it is possible that an employee does not qualify under either of the statutes, in which case, the right to childcare leave (if any) would depend on the contract of employment or collective agreement.

133. Under section 87(A)1 of the Employment Act, an employee who has served an employer for a period of not less than three months and who has any child below the age of 7 years at any time during any relevant period is entitled to childcare leave of two days for that relevant period. This leave applies to both parents, and the amount of leave is the same regardless of the number of children. The 'relevant period' refers to a period of twelve months as agreed to by the employee and his or her employer or where there is no such agreement, a calendar year.[110] However, as mentioned earlier, the Employment Act does not apply to all employees.[111]

134. Under section 12B(1) of the Child Development Co-Savings Act, an employee who has served an employer for a period of not less than three months and has any child below the age of 7 years and who is or becomes a qualifying child at any time during any relevant period, is entitled to childcare leave. The number of days of childcare leave can be up to six days depending on the period of service of the employee with the employer during the relevant period. This leave applies to both parents, and the amount of leave is the same regardless of the number of children. The 'relevant period' refers to a period of twelve months as agreed to by the employee and his or her employer or where there is no such agreement, a calendar year.[112] The term 'qualifying child' is defined in section 12B(21) of the Child Development Co-Savings Act to mean a child who is a citizen of Singapore. The reason why there is a requirement that the child must be a Singapore citizen is to deal with the issue of dwindling birth rates among Singaporeans. Further, in an attempt not to burden employers, pursuant to section 12C of the Child Development Co-Savings Act, when the employer pays, he is entitled to partial reimbursement from the government if the number of childcare leave is four days or more. The Child Development Co-Savings Act applies to all employees, but because of the requirement that the child must be a 'qualifying child', not all employees would qualify under this statute. Under the Child Development Co-Savings Act, it is also possible to claim 'extended' childcare leave amounting to two days in respect of a qualifying child who is above 7 years but below 13 years of age. However, the maximum number of days of childcare leave plus extended childcare leave is six.

135. Under both statutes, it is generally not possible to carry forward the childcare leave.[113] In addition, under both statutes, it is also not possible to get payment in lieu for childcare leave not taken.[114] The leave would also be forfeited if the contract of employment were terminated by either party for whatever reason as provided in sections 87A and 12B of the respective statutes. Also, as provided by these

110. 110.*See* para. 125.
111. *See* para. 10.
112. Section of the Child Development Co-Savings Act.
113. Section 87A(4) of the Employment Act and s. 12B(8) of the Child Development Co-Savings Act.
114. Section 87A(6) of the Employment Act and s. 12B(11) of the Child Development Co-Savings Act.

respective sections, an employer who does not pay or does not grant childcare leave without a reasonable cause will be committing an offence.

§10. Adoption Leave

136. Another type of leave relates to adoption leave which is governed by the Child Development Co-Savings Act. As stated earlier, the Child Development Co-Savings Act applies to all employees. Under section 12A of the Child Development Co-Savings Act, a female employee is entitled to twelve weeks of paid adoption leave, which has to be taken within twelve months of the child's birth. However, there are some preconditions before the adoption leave can be claimed. The female employee must have worked for three months for the employer. Further, the child or the female employee or her husband must be a Singapore citizen. The employer who pays the employee can claim reimbursement from the government, though the amount of reimbursement is subject to a limit.

§11. Trade Union Work-Related Leave

137. Yet another type of leave is the leave for the purposes of carrying out trade unions activities. Under section 81 of the Industrial Relations Act, the employer is obliged to grant leave for a 'reasonable' period for this purpose, and the employer is also obliged to pay during the leave, provided the employee is absent from work to represent members of his trade union in relation to industrial matters pertaining to his employer.

§12. Reservist Leave

138. Another type of leave is a reservist or national service leave, which relates to compulsory military or police service, which is practised in Singapore. Under section 23 of the Enlistment Act, the employer of a person who is required to report for certain services, such as national service, is obliged to grant leave of absence, failure to do so being an offence.

Chapter 5. Remuneration and Other Payments

§1. Background

139. In Singapore, as mentioned previously,[115] there is no national minimum wage, though, for particular sectors (namely, security, landscaping and cleaning), there is a minimum wage. Also, as already mentioned,[116] there are no statutes guaranteeing equal pay or retrenchment benefits. However, under the Employment Act, there are certain provisions relating to salary, which are examined below. Aside from the Employment Act, certain forms of social security as provided in the Central Provident Fund Act and the Work Injury Compensation Act are also explored in this chapter. Reference will also be made to the Skills Development Levy Act under which the employer has to make a particular kind of payment in respect of employees in the form of a levy.

§2. Salary Payment

140. In respect of employees covered by the Employment Act,[117] section 20(2) of that Act provides that the salary period shall not exceed one month. Further section 21(1) of the Employment Act provides that salary earned by an employee under a contract of service other than overtime work has to be paid before the expiry of the seventh day after the last day of the salary period. Section 25 of the Employment Act provides that salary is to be paid during working hours at the place of work or at any other place agreed between the employer and employee, though that section allows payment to be credited into the employee's Singapore bank account as well. As a matter of practice, the last-mentioned method is the most common mode of payment. Breach of these provisions results in the commission of an offence under section 34. For employees covered by the Employment Act, it is also necessary to issue a payslip pursuant to section 96A.

141. For employees not covered by the Employment Act, these matters have to be determined by looking at the express or implied terms of the contract, though it is likely to be an implied term that salary must be paid within a reasonable time. This aside, in the case of foreign employees employed on work passes (for instance, a domestic worker who is not covered by the Employment Act), the conditions[118] subject to which their work passes were issued would also contain provisions relating to payment, breach of which conditions would also result in the commission of an offence.[119]

---

115. *See* para. 75.
116. *See* paras 81 and 77.
117. *See* para. 10.
118. *See* para. 47.
119. Section 22 of the Employment of Foreign Manpower Act.

§3. Deductions from Salary

142. In respect of employees covered by the Employment Act,[120] section 26 of that Act provides that no deductions can be made from the salary of the employee other than those which are authorized under the Employment Act or those which are permitted by order of a court or other competent authority. A breach of section 26 results in the commission of an offence under section 34 of the Employment Act.

143. The deductions permitted under the Employment Act are set out in section 27. These include a long list such as deductions for absence from work, deductions for damage to or loss of goods or for loss of money, deductions for the actual cost of meals, deductions for house accommodation, deductions for amenities and services, deductions for advances or loans or adjustment of over-payments of salary, deductions for income tax, deductions for the provident fund or other such schemes, deductions for cooperative society dues and deductions approved by the Minister (such as perhaps the payment of union fees). However, there are limits as to the extent of deductions in respect of many of these grounds. For instance, pursuant to section 31 of the Employment Act, the amount of loan or advance that can be deducted cannot exceed one-quarter of the salary for a salary period in respect of which the deduction is made.

144. As for employees not falling under the Employment Act, reference has to be made to the express or implied terms of the contract as to whether such deductions can be made. For instance, the employer may have an implied right to claim back an overpayment of salary subject to some exceptions such as a change of position. Some deductions could also be allowed by virtue of other statutory provisions. For instance, under the Central Provident Fund Act, pursuant to section 7(2) of that statute, the employer can deduct the employee's share of the Central Provident Fund contributions from his salary. In addition, in the case of foreign employees employed on work passes (for instance, a domestic worker who is not covered by the Employment Act), the conditions[121] subject to which their work passes were issued would contain provisions relating to deductions (for instance that levy cannot be deducted), a breach of which would result in the commission of an offence.[122]

§4. Salary Increases

145. Whether an employee is entitled to salary increases depends on the contract or collective agreement. In the absence of an express provision in the contract or collective agreement, the employee may nonetheless negotiate with the employer for salary increases. In this context, reference should be made to the National Wages Council, which is unique to Singapore. This is a tripartite council set up in 1972,

120. *See* para. 10.
121. *See* para. 47.
122. Section 22 of the Employment of Foreign Manpower Act.

the function of which is to meet annually to make recommendations as to the direction in which wages should go. Based on this, employers and employees may carry out their negotiations. This is especially the case with regards to unionized companies.

§5. Bonuses

146. In relation to bonuses, whether they are payable depends on the contractual terms or the collective agreement. However, in Singapore, if the contract describes the bonus to be discretionary as opposed to guaranteed, whether the employer's decision not to pay can be challenged is not entirely clear following a recent High Court decision.[123] In addition, under the Employment Act, for employees falling under the Employment Act,[124] there is a prohibition against contracts or collective agreements providing for annual wage supplements which cover a period longer than one month.[125] The idea behind this prohibition is to encourage the payment of bonuses based on performance rather than making bonuses automatic entitlements regardless of performance.

§6. Person Who Has to Pay Salary

147. The person who is liable to pay the salary will obviously be the employer. However, for employees covered under the Employment Act,[126] section 65 provides where a principal in the course of or for the purposes of or in pursuance of his trade or business, contracts with a contractor for the supply of labour or for the execution by the contractor of the whole or any part of the work undertaken by the principal, and any salary is due to any workman[127] by the contractor (or any subcontractor under the contractor for labour supplied), the principal and the contractor and any such contractor (not being the employer) can be jointly and severally liable with the employer for the payment of the workman. Thus, the workman who does work and is not paid receives some protection under this section, though the liability is limited to one month's salary by virtue of section 65(1A). The person who pays pursuant to this section can, in turn, institute an action against the employer to seek reimbursement as provided in section 65(3) of the Employment Act.

§7. Central Provident Fund

148. Pensions are not common in Singapore and are restricted to certain public officers. Thus, the main form of social security for most employees in Singapore is

123. Compare *Latham Scott v. Credit Suisse First Boston* [2000] 2 SLR (R) 30 and *Leong Hin Chuee v. Citra Group Pte Ltd* [2015] 2 SLR 603.
124. *See* para. 10.
125. Section 48 of the Employment Act.
126. *See* para. 10.
127. As to definition of 'workman' *see* para. 14.

the Central Provident Fund. Under section 7 of the Central Provident Fund Act, unless exempted, every employer of an employee has to make contributions at the appropriate rates to the fund in respect of that employee on a monthly basis. Failure to make payment within the prescribed period results in the commission of an offence under section 58 of the Central Provident Fund Act.

149. The Central Provident Fund scheme was started in 1955, and its main aim was to provide for compulsory savings which could be used upon retirement. However, since its inception, various sub-schemes have been introduced, which allow the monies to be used for various matters such as the purchase of a home or medical insurance, even before retirement.

I. The Minimum Amount and Employees Covered

150. As reflected in the First Schedule to the Central Provident Fund Act, the minimum amount of salary which would trigger the obligation to contribute to the fund in any month is SGD 50.

However, under the Central Provident Fund Act, there are various exemptions when such contributions need not be paid, as already mentioned previously.[128] This is pursuant to the Central Provident Fund (Exemptions – Miscellaneous) (Consolidation) Order and other related orders. For instance, contributions need not be paid in respect of domestic employees and all employees who are not Singapore citizens or permanent residents. In addition, as a matter of practice, contributions are not required for employees who are posted overseas or who are on study leave overseas.

II. Amount Payable

151. The amount of contribution payable is set out in the First Schedule to the Central Provident Fund Act and varies according to the age of the employee, the amount of salary earned and whether the employee is a citizen or a permanent resident. Lower rates are payable in respect of permanent residents within the first two years of obtaining permanent residency. This is to allow both the employee (who could have less take-home pay) and the employer (who would have to pay more) to ease gradually into the system.

152. In relation to an employee earning more than SGD 1,500 per month and who is not more than 50 years of age and who is a citizen, the First Schedule provides that a contribution amounting to 37% of the ordinary wages (subject to a stated maximum of SGD) and 37% of the additional wages for a month has to be paid. However, pursuant to section 7(2) of the Central Provident Fund Act, a sum equivalent to 20% of the ordinary wages (subject to a stated maximum which is currently SGD 1,000) and 20% of the additional wages for a month can be recovered

128. *See* para. 16.

from the employee himself. Though there is no separate salary limit for additional wages, there is a salary limit for ordinary wages and additional wages taken together (namely, SGD 102,000 per year).

153. The term 'ordinary wages' refers to remuneration due or granted wholly or exclusively in respect of employment during that month and payable before the due date for the payment of the contribution for that month. Thus, for instance, salary and allowances which are payable monthly would amount to ordinary wages. 'Additional wages' refer to remuneration other than ordinary wages, such as bonuses which are not referable to any particular month.

154. The term 'wages' is defined in section 2 of the Central Provident Fund Act, and it means remuneration in money, including any bonus due or granted to a person in respect of employment. In *PN Electronic Pte Ltd v. Public Prosecutor*,[129] the court held that the term 'remuneration' meant a reward for services rendered. Thus, on the facts of the case, reimbursement of travel expenses incurred from home to work did not amount to 'wages' as it was not a reward for services rendered. For similar reasons, reimbursements for work-related entertainment expenses or laundry expenses are unlikely to amount to a reward for services rendered and hence are not likely to attract a contribution. Likewise, matters such as salary in lieu of notice or retrenchment benefits are unlikely to be considered to be a reward for services rendered and hence too; these are not likely to attract a contribution. On the other hand, payments which are a reward for services rendered such as payment of overtime pay or payment for holiday leave not taken would attract a contribution. In *Ponggol Marina Pte Ltd v. Central Provident Fund Board*,[130] for instance, the court held that meal allowances were a reward for services rendered, and they supplemented the employee's wages. Hence, contributions had to be made in respect of them.

§8. Work Injury Compensation Act

155. Another statute that may require an employer to make payment is the Work Injury Compensation Act. The Work Injury Compensation Act applies to all employees. However, there are some exceptions that have been discussed previously.[131] Once an employee is covered, it does not matter that he is a foreigner or part-timer. Once covered, it is also not possible to contractually exclude liability arising under this statute as a result of section 23 of the Work Injury Compensation Act.

129. [1985] 1 MLJ 279.
130. [2001] 2 SLR (R) 769.
131. *See* para. 15.

I. Persons Liable to Pay

156. Under the Work Injury Compensation Act, the liability to pay compensation is primarily placed on the employer, and the term 'employer' is defined in section 2 of the Work Injury Compensation Act to include the government and any statutory board. Further, the above definition provides that the employer continues to be liable even where his employee is temporarily 'lent' or 'let on hire' to another person. However, aside from the employer, under the Work Injury Compensation Act, the principal can also be liable. In this regard, section 13(1) provides that where a person (i.e., the principal), in the course of or for the purpose of his trade or business contracts with any other person (i.e., the employer) for the execution by the employer of the whole or any part of any work, or for the supply of labour to carry out any work, undertaken by the principal, the principal shall be liable to pay any employee employed in the execution of the work, any compensation which he would have been liable to pay as if the employee had been immediately employed by him. The principal who pays can get an indemnity from the employer by virtue of section 13(3) of the Work Injury Compensation Act.

II. Personal Injury by Accident

157. For there to be liability under the Work Injury Compensation Act, section 7(1) provides that there has to be a personal injury by accident arising out of and in the course of employment.

158. The phrase 'arising out of' suggests that there must be some connection between the employment and the injury. Thus, for instance, in *NTUC Income Insurance Co-operative Ltd v. Next of Kin of Narayasamy*,[132] where a coachman suffered a heart attack while loading bags onto a coach, the court held that there was such a connection and hence compensation was payable.

159. The phrase 'in the course of employment' suggests the injury must occur to the employee while he is doing what a man so employed may reasonably be doing and while he was at a place where he could reasonably be expected to be. In this regard, generally travelling to and from work would not be in the course of employment unless the employee is obliged by the terms of his contract to use a particular mode of transport and the accident occurs while using that particular mode. Thus, in *QBE Insurance (International) Ltd v. Julaiha Bee*,[133] where the employee concerned died in a road accident while travelling to his place of work on a motorcycle, it was held compensation was not payable as it was not compulsory for him to own a motorcycle and come to work in a motorcycle. Nonetheless, section 8(1) of the Work Injury Compensation Act sets out certain situations which are deemed to arise out of and in the course of employment. One such situation relates to an accident happening to an employee while he is travelling as a passenger by any

132. [2006] 4 SLR (R) 507.
133. [1991] 2 SLR (R) 724.

means of transport to or from his place of work with the express or implied permission of his employer, which transport is operated by or on behalf of his employer or by some other person in pursuance of an arrangement made with his employer and is not being operated in the ordinary course of public transport service.

160. While section 8(1) of the Work Injury Compensation Act sets out some situations where compensation would be payable, section 7(2) of the Work Injury Compensation Act sets out certain situations where compensation will not be payable. Section 7(2) provides that there will be no liability if the injury is directly attributable to the employee having been made under the influence of alcohol or a drug not prescribed by a medical practitioner or if the incapacity or death results from deliberate self-injury or deliberate aggravation of an accidental injury. Further, under section 3(5), an employer is not obliged to pay compensation in respect of any injury to an employee suffered in a fight or attempted assault on one or more persons. However, the subsections provide several exceptions, such as where the employee did not assault or attempt to assault any person in the fight or attempted assault or did assault any such person in the exercise of the right of private defence as recognized in the Penal Code.

III. Occupational Diseases

161. Aside from personal injury by accident arising out of and in the course of employment, under section 10(1) of the Work Injury Compensation Act, if an employee employed in any occupation specified in the second column of the Second Schedule to that Act contracts an occupational disease specified in the first column of that Schedule opposite that occupation or an employee who has been employed in that occupation contracts that disease within the period specified in the third column of that Schedule opposite that occupation after ceasing to be so employed, and the incapacity or death of the employee results from that disease, compensation shall be payable as if the disease were a personal injury by accident arising out of and in the course of that employment. The diseases covered in the Second Schedule include diseases such as tuberculosis, poisoning by certain agents, occupational skin cancer and other skin diseases, occupational asthma and noise-induced deafness.

162. Further pursuant to section 10(1)c, if an employee contracts a disease which is not specified in the first column of the Second Schedule but which is directly attributable to an exposure arising out of and in the course of employment to a chemical or biological agent and the incapacity or death of the employee results from that disease, compensation can also be claimed.

IV. Insurance

163. In order to deal with such potential liability, it is compulsory for the employer to take out and maintain insurance coverage as provided in section 24 of the Work Injury Compensation Act.

164. However, there is a major exception to this rule. Under the Work Injury Compensation (Insurance) Regulations, the requirement to maintain insurance is waived in respect of the government and employers of all persons with monthly earnings exceeding SGD 2,100 (SGD 2,600 from April 2021) and who are employed otherwise than by way of manual labour. The government is excluded as it will have the funds to meet any potential liability and the other exception relates to the situation where the risk of an accident or injury occurring is low. This is another illustration of how in Singapore, the law relating to employment tries to balance the competing interests of the various parties involved.

V. No Double Compensation

165. An employee may claim compensation under the Work Injury Compensation or sue the party responsible for the injury under some other area of law, such as a breach of a duty of care.[134] He cannot claim both as provided for in section 63 of the Work Injury Compensation Act, or else he would be doubly enriched.

166. There are differences between the two avenues. If the employee claims under Work Injury Compensation Act, the compensation is subject to a certain limit,[135] but fault need not be established. On the other hand, if the employee sues for a breach of duty of care, fault has to be established, though there is no limit as to compensation. In addition, there is a difference in relation to the time limit. In the case of work injury compensation, it is one year pursuant to section 39 of the Work Injury Compensation Act, whereas, in the case of negligence causing personal injury, it is three years pursuant to section 24A(2) of the Limitation Act.

VI. Amount of Compensation Payable

167. The amount of compensation payable varies depending on whether the permanent incapacity or death results or temporary incapacity results. The First Schedule to the Work Injury Compensation Act lists injuries that are deemed to be permanent and the extent to which the earning capacity is lost. Where permanent incapacity or death results, the amount of compensation payable is arrived at by multiplying the monthly earnings of the employee by an appropriate factor set out in the Third Schedule, which is worked out on the basis of the age of the employee. The younger the employee, the more he will get considering that he would have

134. *See* para. 69.
135. *See* para. 167.

more wasted years ahead. However, there is a maximum and minimum amount as provided in the Third Schedule to the Work Injury Compensation Act. In the case of death, the maximum is currently SGD 225,000, and the minimum is SGD 76,000. In the case of permanent incapacity, the maximum is currently SGD 289,000, and the minimum is SGD 97,000.

168. In the case of temporary incapacity, as provided in the Third Schedule to the Work Injury Compensation Act, the employee is entitled to his full earnings for a period of sixty days if he is hospitalized and if he is not hospitalized, for a period of fourteen days. Further, he is entitled to a periodical payment of an amount equal to two-thirds of his earnings during the incapacity or during a period of one year, whichever is shorter.

169. Aside from compensation, again under the Third Schedule to the Work Injury Compensation Act, the employer is also obliged to bear the cost of medical treatment. However, there is a limit which is currently SGD 45,000.

§9. Skills Development Levy

170. Another interesting aspect of the employer's obligation in Singapore is the Skills Development Levy which is required to be paid under the Skills Development Levy Act. The basic idea of the levy is to encourage employers to send their employees (especially lower-level employees) for skills upgrading and training.

171. The levy is payable in respect of all employees other than domestic employees. As set out in section 3 of the Skills Development Levy Act, the rate of the levy is 0.25% of the remuneration in any month or at the rate of SGD 2, whichever is greater. However, the maximum amount of salary per month that would attract a levy is SGD 4,500, and hence the maximum of the levy in respect of any employee is at most SGD 11.25 per month. As provided in section 3 of the Skills Development Levy Act, any levy owing can be claimed as a debt due by the Agency responsible for the collection of the Levy (which is the Central Provident Fund Board) and making false returns is an offence under section 11 of the Skills Development Levy Act.

172. While the employer has to contribute and can make use of the Fund, it is not compulsory for him to make use of it. Further, there is no correlation between the amount contributed by the employer and the amount of funding he can obtain under the scheme. However, it should also be highlighted that subsidies under the Fund, as a matter of practice, apply when the employers send employees who are citizens or permanent residents (as opposed to foreigners) for skills upgrading and training.

Chapter 6. Termination of Employment

§1. Introduction

173. A contract of employment can come to an end in one of four ways, namely, by performance, by frustration, by agreement or by the repudiatory or fundamental breach. It is also possible that more than one way applies to any given set of facts.

§2. Performance

174. In relation to performance, under a contract, both parties undertake to do something, and when that something has been done, the contract comes to an end by performance. Thus, for instance, if an employee is hired on a two-year contract and the employee works for those two years during which he is paid, at the end of those two years, the contract would come to an end by performance unless it is renewed. In this connection, though not entirely clear, it is likely that the employer is not under any implied obligation to renew the contract.

§3. Frustration

175. The next way in which the contract can come to an end is by frustration. Frustration refers to the occurrence of an event after the making of the contract, which makes the further performance of the contract impossible or radically different.[136] Thus, for instance, the employment contract may be frustrated by the death of the employee. Sickness of the employee too may result in frustration, but whether frustration does result in such a situation depends on many factors such as the nature of the illness and the past period of employment with that employer. It is possible that imprisonment too results in frustration depending on factors such as the length of imprisonment and the importance of getting someone else to do the job in the meantime. Frustration can also arise from events relating to the employer. For instance, the impossibility brought about by war or invasion may result in frustration.

176. If frustration does occur, the contract automatically comes to an end without either party having to give notice or salary in lieu of notice. As to the effect on payments due or payable, such issues are governed by the Frustrated Contracts Act. However, to date, there have not been any reported cases in Singapore relating to frustration or the Frustrated Contracts Act in the context of an employment contract.

136. *See*, for instance, *RDC Concrete Pte Ltd v. Sato Kogyo (S) Pte Ltd* [2007] 4 SLR (R) 413.

§4. AGREEMENT

177. The third way in which the contract can come to an end is by agreement. In this regard, a distinction has to be made between employees falling under the Employment Act[137] and employees not falling under the Act.

I. Notice

178. In relation to employees falling under the Employment Act, section 10(1) of that Act provides that either party may terminate the contract by giving notice. The amount of notice to be given is as follows:

- one day's notice if the employee has been employed for less than twenty-six weeks;
- one week's notice if the employee has been employed for twenty-six weeks or more but less than two years;
- two weeks' notice if the employee has been employed for two years or more but less than five years; and
- four weeks' notice if the employee has been employed for five years or more.

179. However, it is possible for the contract to provide for a shorter period of notice even if the employee falls under the Employment Act as provided in section 10(2). Nonetheless, the period of notice must be the same for the employer and the employee also as provided in section 10(2). By virtue of section 10(5) of the Employment Act, the notice has to be in writing. If the notice is not in writing, it is likely that the notice will be null and void. Also, as provided in section 10(5) of the Employment Act, the notice can be given at any time. It is also likely that the party receiving the notice does not have to accept it in order for it to be effective.

180. For employees not falling under the Employment Act, there could be an express clause governing the amount of notice to be given, which is very common as a matter of practice. However, unlike under the Employment Act, it is possible for the contract to provide that the notice to be given by the employer is different from that to be given by the employee.

181. If there is no express provision, there is an implied provision that either party may be able to terminate the contract by giving reasonable notice.[138] What is reasonable notice would depend on factors such as the qualifications of the employee and the length of employment prior to the termination. For instance, in *Ng Peng Hon Stanley v. AAF Pte Ltd*,[139] considering the fact that the employee in question was a manager of a company, it was held that three months' notice would have been appropriate on the facts.

137. *See* para. 10.
138. *D'Cruz v. Seafield Amalgamated Rubber Co Ltd* (1963) MLJ 154.
139. [1977–1978] SLR (R) 460.

182. However, there are some limited exceptions to the implied right to terminate by giving reasonable notice. For instance, if it is a fixed-term contract and the parties did not envisage an earlier termination, there may not be an implied right to terminate the contract earlier.

183. For employees not covered by the Employment Act, the notice does not have to be in writing unless the contract states so. Where there is a contractual requirement for the notice to be in writing and it is not, it is likely that the notice is null and void. It is also likely that the notice can be given at any time unless the contract has a provision to the contrary. It is also likely that the party receiving the notice does not have to accept it in order for it to be effective.

II. Salary in Lieu of Notice

184. Aside from giving notice, it may also be possible for the contract to be terminated by salary in lieu of notice.

185. For employees falling under the Employment Act, either party has the right to give salary in lieu of notice by virtue of section 11(1) of that Act.

186. For employees not falling under the Employment Act, there could be an express clause in the contract which allows either or one party to terminate the contract by paying salary in lieu of notice. As a matter of practice, this is indeed very common. If there is no such express clause, the employee may not have an implied right to terminate the contract by notice as a sudden departure could cause hardship to the employer. As for the employer, following the case of *Hengxin Technology Ltd v. Jiang Wei*,[140] it is likely that he too may not have an implied right to terminate by giving salary in lieu of notice unless he can establish that the employee would not be in a worse financial situation even if the employer terminated the contract by salary in lieu of notice as opposed to notice.

187. The above rules relating to termination by notice or salary in lieu of notice also apply to part-timers and probationary employees. In relation to probationary employees, it may also be highlighted that generally, there is no assurance that the probation would continue until the end of the probationary period, and it is possible for the employer to terminate the contract even before the probationary period.[141] In addition, in the event that the employer does not confirm the employee at the end of the probationary period but just continues with the employment as before, it will be deemed that the employee is continuing his probation.[142]

140. Suit No. 161 of 2008, Singapore High Court, unreported.
141. *See John Wisdom v. Roebourne Finance and Investment Co Ltd* [1928] SSLR 65.
142. *See Lai Swee Lin Linda v. Attorney-General*, Suit No 995 of 2004, Singapore High Court, unreported.

III. Generally, Termination Need Not Be for a Just Cause

188. In relation to termination by notice or salary in lieu of notice, one important question is whether the employer (or the employee, for that matter) must terminate the contract in good faith. Currently, as the law stands, there is no such requirement.[143] It may also be noted that Singapore has not ratified the International Labour Organization's Termination of Employment Convention (No. 158). However, there are some statutory protections that are discussed below. Nonetheless, taken as a whole, Singapore does not have strong unfair dismissal laws in place, probably the main concern being the impact on businesses.

IV. Exceptions Where There Must Be a Just Cause

189. One exception to the rule that termination does not have to be in good faith is set out in section 14(2) of the Employment Act. Section 14(2) provides that where an employee considers that he has been dismissed without just cause or excuse by his employer, he may lodge a claim with the Employment Claims Tribunal. The term 'dismiss' is defined in section 2(1) of the Employment Act to mean the termination of the contract of service of an employee by his employer, with or without notice and whether on the grounds of misconduct or otherwise. Constructive dismissals are now also covered. However, though not entirely clear, the term 'dismiss' is unlikely to cover a non-renewal of a contract of employment. The time limit for making a claim is one month. There is also a compulsory requirement to have prior mediation. If mediation is not successful, the matter can proceed to the Employment Claims Tribunal, which can order compensation or reinstatement.

190. Another exception is set out in section 35(3) of the Industrial Relations Act, and it is similar to section 14(2) of the Employment Act. However, one difference is that this section applies to unionized employees, and the employee has to bring the claim through his union. Another difference is that the term 'dismiss' is not defined under the Industrial Relations Act, and so it is not clear whether it covers termination of the contract by notice or salary in lieu of notice, though it is likely that it does.

191. Yet another exception is set out in section 81 of the Employment Act, which relates to absence due to maternity leave.[144] Section 81 provides that it is unlawful for the employer to give a female employee notice of dismissal during her leave of absence or on such a day that the notice will expire during her absence. As mentioned, the term 'dismiss' is defined in section 2(1) of the Employment Act to mean the termination of the contract of service of an employee by his employer, with or without notice and whether on the grounds of misconduct or otherwise. Thus termination by notice (or salary in lieu of notice) is also covered. However, though

143. *See D'Cruz v. Seafield Amalgamated Rubber Co Ltd* (1963) MLJ 154.

144. The same protection applies in relation to employees claiming maternity leave under the Child Development Co-Savings Act by virtue of s. 12(1) of that statute.

not entirely clear, the term 'dismiss' is unlikely to cover a non-renewal of a contract of employment. Breach of section 81 results in the commission of an offence under section 87 of the Employment Act. A dismissal in breach of section 81 is likely to be null and void, though this is not expressly stated in the statute.

192. However, there are two exceptions to section 81 as provided in the section itself. The first is section 84[145] of the Employment Act, which provides that the employer is entitled to give notice of dismissal where is sufficient cause for the dismissal at any point of her pregnancy. Where the employee feels that she has been dismissed in breach of section 84, she may refer the matter to the Minister within two months of her dismissal. The term 'Minister' refers to the Minister of Manpower in this context. Pursuant to section 84(3), the Minister, if he is satisfied that the dismissal is without sufficient cause, may order reinstatement or the payment of compensation.

193. Another exception is section 84A of the Employment Act.[146] Section 84A provides that if notice of dismissal on the ground of redundancy has been given at any time during pregnancy, though the termination itself would be effective, the female employee would be entitled to any maternity payment she would statutorily have been entitled to if not for the redundancy. This is another illustration of how in Singapore, the law relating to employment tries to balance the interest of the various parties involved.

194. Another exception to the rule that the termination does not have to be for a just cause is set out in the Retirement and Re-employment Act. Under section 4(2) of the Retirement and Re-employment Act, dismissal before the age of 62, or such other age as may be prescribed by the Minister, on the ground of age, results in the commission of an offence on the part of the employer. By virtue of section 8 of the Retirement and Re-employment Act, an employee who considered that he has been dismissed in breach of section 4(2) may, within one month of the dismissal, make a representation to the Minister who may then order reinstatement and/or compensation. The term 'dismissal' is defined in section 2(2) of the Retirement and Re-employment Act, and it covers termination by notice or salary in lieu of notice and constructive dismissal. Though not entirely clear, arguably, it also covers the non-renewal of a contract of employment. All employees are covered under the Retirement and Re-employment Act. However, as established in *Noor Mohamed Bin Mumtaz Shah v. Apollo Enterprises Ltd*,[147] if the employee is dismissed because of poor performance and not age, then section 4(2) of the Retirement and Re-employment Act would not be applicable.

---

145. *Ibid.*
146. *Ibid.*
147. [2000] 1 SLR (R) 670.

195. Under the Retirement and Re-employment Act, as already discussed,[148] the employer also has an obligation to offer re-employment under certain circumstances after retirement up to the age of 65 (or such other age as may be prescribed by the Minister). An employee who is dismissed during this interim period without a just cause or excuse may, within one month after the last day of his employment with his employer, notify the Commissioner of Labour pursuant to section 8A of the Retirement and Re-employment Act. Conciliation proceedings will take place, and if they are not successful, the employee can then make representations to the Minister within one month of the conclusion of the conciliation proceedings as provided in section 8B of the Retirement and Re-employment Act. Also, as provided in section 8B of the Retirement and Re-employment Act, the Minister has the power to order reinstatement or compensation and the failure to comply with the directions of the Minister results in the commission of an offence.

196. Aside from all these, there are also other protections against unfair dismissal in very specific situations such as dismissal, which is connected with national service (under section 22 of the Enlistment Act) or the reporting of health and safety breaches at work (under section 18 of the Workplace Safety and Health Act) and dismissal which is discriminatory in nature based on union work or membership (under section 82 of the Industrial Relations Act).

§5. Repudiatory or Fundamental Breach

197. Another way in which the contract of employment can come to an end is by a repudiatory or fundamental breach committed by the employer or employee. In such an event, the contract can be terminated on the spot by the innocent party without having to give notice or salary in lieu of notice if he so wishes.

I. What Amounts to a Repudiatory or Fundamental Breach

198. The leading case on repudiatory or fundamental breach is *RDC Concrete Pte Ltd v. Sato Kogyo (S) Pte Ltd*,[149] though the case did not relate to employment law as such.

In this case, the court held that the first thing to consider was whether the contract clearly and unambiguously provided for the event or events pursuant to which the innocent party was entitled to terminate the contract. If so, the contract was terminated. An example would be a clause in the contract, which provides that if the employee is convicted of a crime, the employer could terminate the contract on the spot without notice or salary in lieu of notice.

199. Second, assuming the contract does not clearly and unambiguously give one party the right to terminate the contract on the happening of certain events, it

148. *See* para. 98.
149. [2007] 4 SLR (R) 413.

would have to be determined whether any party to the contract has by his words or conduct renounced the contract, that is, has clearly conveyed to the other party that he will not perform his contractual obligations at all. In such an event too, the innocent party can terminate the contract on the spot without notice or salary in lieu of notice. For instance, if an employee does not turn up for work after signing an employment contract, this could amount to such renunciation.

200. Third, depending on the nature of the term breached, the innocent party may have a right to terminate the contract summarily without notice or salary in lieu of notice. There are basically two types of the term. The first is the condition. A condition is a term which the parties have intended to be so important that any breach of it (regardless of the actual consequences of the breach) would entitle the innocent party to terminate the contract on the spot without notice or salary in lieu of notice. The second is the warranty. A warranty is a term in which the parties have intended that no breach of which will ever entitle the innocent party to terminate the contract on the spot without notice or salary in lieu of notice (though the innocent party could sue for damages). Whether a term is a condition or warranty would have to be determined at the time of contracting. By way of illustration, a clause requiring the maintenance of confidentiality is more likely to be a condition, whereas a clause relating to office attire is more likely to be a warranty. However, much depends on the actual facts and further, in many situations, the intention of the parties would not easily point towards a term being a condition or warranty.

201. Fourth, assuming a term cannot be classified as a condition or warranty or even if it is a warranty, if the nature and consequences of the breach deprive the innocent party of substantially the whole benefit which was intended that he should have under the contract, then too the innocent party can terminate the contract on the spot without notice or salary in lieu of notice. Whether the breach is of such a serious nature would depend on many factors such as the nature of the contract, the relationship it creates and whether damages would provide an adequate remedy. To give an illustration, in *Motilal v. Gutherie Agency (M) Ltd*,[150] where the employee in question misappropriated rents due to his employer for himself, the court held that his summary dismissal was justified.

202. In relation to employees covered under the Employment Act,[151] reference must be made to sections 11(2), 14(1) and 13. Section 11(2) of the Employment Act allows either party to terminate the contract summarily if there is a wilful breach by the other. Section 13(1) of the Employment Act provides that an employer shall be deemed to have broken his contract of service if he does pay salary in accordance with Part II of the Employment Act. Section 13(2) of the Employment Act provides that an employee shall be deemed to have broken his contract of service if he has been continuously absent from work for more than two days without prior leave from his employer or without reasonable excuse or without informing or attempting to inform his employer of the excuse for such absence. 'Deemed to have broken' in

150. [1968] 1 MLJ 211.
151. *See* para. 10.

this context means that that party has committed a repudiatory breach which would allow the innocent party to terminate the contract on the spot as established in *Arokiasamy Joseph Clement Louis v. Singapore Airlines*.[152] Section 14(2) of the Employment Act allows the employer to terminate the contract summarily if the employee is guilty of misconduct. Though the Employment Act provides for some situations whereby the contract can be terminated summarily, it is likely that the sections are not meant to be exhaustive in that if a breach is likely to be considered fundamental or repudiatory in common law (for instance, possibly sexual harassment), then, it is likely that the innocent party can still terminate the contract summarily.

II. Suspension

203. Where the employee has committed a repudiatory or fundamental breach, the employer may wish to suspend the employee instead of dismissing him.

204. For employees not covered under the Employment Act, if the employer wishes to suspend the employee without pay, this has to be provided for by the contract of employment. However, the employer can always suspend the employee with pay.

205. In the case of employees falling under the Employment Act,[153] pursuant to section 14(1)b of the Employment Act, the employer may, instead of dismissing an employee for misconduct after a due inquiry, suspend him from work without payment of salary for a period not exceeding a week. For employees falling under the Employment Act, the employer may also suspend the employee for a period not exceeding one week (unless the permission of the Commissioner is sought to suspend for a longer period) during the inquiry as provided in section 14(8) of that Act.

III. Procedure for Summary Dismissal

206. In terms of the procedure for summary dismissal of the employees, for employees not falling under the Employment Act, there is no procedure to be followed unless the contract of employment provides for it, which is not common as a matter of practice. Hence usually, there is no necessity to give the employee a chance to be heard.[154]

207. However, in respect of employees falling under the Employment Act,[155] section 14(1) provides that an employee can be dismissed without notice for misconduct only after a 'due inquiry'. If it turns out that there is no 'due inquiry', the remedy would be damages and not reinstatement as established in *Lim Tow Peng v.*

152. [2004] 2 SLR (R) 233.
153. *See* para. 10.
154. *See Vasudevan Pillai v. The City Council of Singapore* [1968–1970] SLR (R) 100.
155. *See* para. 10.

Singapore Bus Services Ltd.[156] However, the requirement to have a due inquiry only relates to dismissal on the grounds of misconduct.

208. There are also some procedures to be followed in relation to public officers under the Constitution and the Public Service (Disciplinary Proceedings) Regulations and in relation to police officers under the Police Force Act and the Police Regulations.

§6. Remedies for Wrongful Dismissal

209. As mentioned earlier,[157] the employer does not have to have a just cause for terminating the contract of employment, though there are some statutory exceptions[158] to this rule. Insofar as some statutory exception applies, whether compensation is payable or whether reinstatement is possible would depend on the statute in question. However, in general, the compensation awarded under the statutory schemes is quite conservative, and reinstatement is not a common remedy.

210. Wrongful dismissal can also take place outside the statutory schemes pertaining to unfair dismissal. For instance, if the employer does not give the correct amount of notice or salary in lieu of notice or thinks that the employee has committed a repudiatory or fundamental breach and hence terminates the contract of the employee summarily without notice or salary in lieu when in effect there is no such breach, the employer could be liable in damages.

211. Outside of the statutory schemes, the amount of damages that would be payable in such a situation would depend on how the contract could have been lawfully terminated: *Chiam Heng Hsien v. Jurong Town Corp.*[159] For instance, if the contract could have been lawfully terminated by giving two months' notice, when in effect it was terminated without any such notice, at most, the employee would be entitled to the salary he would have earned during the two months. Salary in this context refers to what the employee would legally have been entitled to receive under his contract during that period. Thus, for instance, if there is a contractual entitlement to a company vehicle or to the services of chauffer or medical check-ups, the loss arising from these can be claimed: *Goh Kim Hai Edward v. Pacific Can Investment Holdings Ltd.*[160] However, as the law stands, the employee would not be able to sue for damages for distress or disappointment or for injured feelings: *Arul Chandran v. Gartshore.*[161] In addition, the employee is expected to minimize or

156. [1974–1976] SLR (R) 673.
157. *See* para. 188.
158. *See* paras 189 onwards.
159. [1985–1986] SLR (R) 92.
160. [1996] 1 SLR (R) 540.
161. [2000] 1 SLR (R) 436.

mitigate his losses, for instance, by getting another suitable job, failing which damages may be reduced.[162] Reinstatement is also generally not awarded for wrongful termination or dismissal in this context as well.[163]

162. *Chiam Heng Hsien v. Jurong Town Corp* [1985–1986] SLR (R) 92.
163. *Lim Tow Peng v. Singapore Bus Services Ltd* [1974–1976] SLR (R) 30.

Chapter 7. Covenants of Non-competition

212. Generally, parties to the contract can agree to whatever terms they want to, the concept of freedom of contract being sacrosanct. However, there are exceptions to this rule.[164] One relates to non-compete and other such restraint of trade clauses. Such clauses may be against public policy, and hence they may not be valid. Whether they are valid depends on whether they are reasonable. This has two distinct angles; namely, the clause must be reasonable as between the parties, and the clause must be reasonable considering the public interest.[165] Reasonableness has to be judged at the time when the contract was entered into.[166]

§1. Reasonable Between the Parties

213. To be reasonable between the parties, first, the employer must have a legitimate interest to be protected.[167] Legitimate interest can cover matters such as trade secrets and highly confidential information or trade connections.[168]

214. Trade secrets or highly confidential information can include non-technical and non-scientific matters. However, it does not include skills, experience and general know-how.[169]

215. In relation to trade connections, this can relate to customers. For the employer to have a legitimate interest in this regard, the employee subject to the restraint must have had personal knowledge and influence over the customers of the employer, and the employee must have been able to leverage the connection in some way.[170]

216. Trade connections can also relate to other employees in the employer's organization. Whether the employer has a legitimate interest in this connection depends on many factors, such as whether the employee subject to the restraint was in a position to influence other employees and whether that employee had confidential information relating to the other employees (such as salary).[171]

217. However, even if the employer has a legitimate interest, the covenant must not be unreasonably wide in order to be reasonable between the parties.[172] The covenant cannot be too wide in terms of area, time and scope of restriction. In relation

164. *See* para. 28.
165. *Man Financial (S) Pte Ltd v. Wong Bark Chuan David* [2008] 1 SLR (R) 663.
166. *Ibid.*
167. *Ibid.*
168. *Ibid.*
169. *Stratech Systems Ltd v. Nyam Chiu Shin*[2005] 2 SLR (R) 579.
170. *Man Financial (S) Pte Ltd v. Wong Bark Chuan David* [2008] 1 SLR (R) 663.
171. *Ibid.*
172. *Ibid.*

to time, the longest restraint that has been upheld in Singapore is three years.[173] In relation to area, a restraint that restricts competition to the whole of Singapore may be valid,[174] but one which is worldwide may be less likely to be reasonable. In relation to scope, much depends on the actual circumstances, but by way of illustration in *Buckman Laboratories (Asia) Pte Ltd v. Lee Wei Hoong,* [175] the plaintiff had business interests in many industries, whereas the defendant, who was an employee of the plaintiff, was employed only in the pulp and paper industry. Nonetheless, the restraint extended to all of the plaintiff's many industries. This was held to be too wide, and hence the restraint of trade clause was not upheld.

218. If a clause is too wide, it may be possible to run a 'blue pencil' through it to sever the unreasonable parts.[176] However, this will only be done where there is no altering or adding of words and where there are no grammatical difficulties. Further, the removal of the unreasonable part must not so change the character of the contract that it becomes not the sort of contract the parties entered into at all.[177] Though this has not been successfully invoked often as a matter of practice in Singapore, there have been occasions when it has been. For instance, in *SeaCAD Technologies Pte Ltd v. Tan Siew Meng* Aaron,[178] the restraint, which originally extended to Malaysia and Singapore, being too wide, was severed using the 'blue pencil' mechanism to restrict it to Singapore.

§2. Reasonable in Public Interest

219. In addition to being reasonable between the parties, for the clause to be valid, it has to be reasonable with reference to public interest.[179] For instance, if the employer is running a monopoly and the employee seeks to set up a competing business, it might be in the interest of the public that such competition be allowed, and hence in such a situation, the restraint of trade clause may not be enforced, even if it is reasonable between the parties.[180]

§3. Remedies

220. Assuming the clause is valid, it may be enforced by means of an injunction. It may also be possible to get an interlocutory injunction. It is also possible for the employer to sue the employee for damages for any losses caused as a result of a breach.

173. *Class Medical Centre Pte Ltd v. Ng Boon Ching* [2010] 2 SLR 386.
174. *Heller Factoring (Singapore) Ltd v. Ng Tong Yang* [1993] 1 SLR (R) 205.
175. [1999] 1 SLR (R) 205.
176. *Man Financial (S) Pte Ltd v. Wong Bark Chuan David* [2008] 1 SLR (R) 663.
177. *Ibid.*
178. Suit No. 250 of 2006, Singapore High Court, unreported.
179. *Man Financial (S) Pte Ltd v. Wong Bark Chuan David* [2008] 1 SLR (R) 663.
180. *Thomas Cowan & Co Ltd v. Orme* [1961] MLJ 41.

§4. Gardening Leave

221. Another way in which the employer may obtain the same result is by placing the employee on gardening leave during the period of notice of termination. Thus, for instance, the contract might provide that instead of a six-month restraint, the employee has to give six months' notice to terminate and that during that time, the employee should not turn up for work but should nonetheless not work for anyone else. The effect is the same, but in this situation, the employer would continue paying the employee for six months. Such clauses tend to be treated more favourably compared to restraint of trade clauses as the employee is being paid and is not deprived of his livelihood. Nonetheless, if such a gardening leave clause is totally unreasonably notwithstanding the payment, it might not be enforceable. There has not been much litigation in Singapore relating to gardening leave clauses (unlike restraint of trade clauses) thus far.

Chapter 8. Settlement of Disputes

222. In relation to employment disputes, as in relation to all other civil disputes, the usual avenues for dispute resolution are open. These include litigation via the normal court system, arbitration and mediation, such as at the Singapore Mediation Centre. Generally, though there is a steady stream of employment law cases handled by the normal court system, the bulk of these tend to be related to work injury claims or negligence claims or claims involving higher management. As for arbitration, it is also becoming a common avenue for dispute resolution for employment matters, especially with regards to higher management.

223. However, in relation to employment matters, there are also other more specific avenues open. These are highlighted below.

§1. Mediation

224. Employees who are union members with collective bargaining rights or at least limited representation rights may approach their unions should there be any employment-related dispute. If the matter cannot be resolved internally, the mediation services of the Ministry of Manpower can again be used.

225. Union members who are executives and who in receipt of salary not exceeding SGD 4,500 a month and who do not have collective bargaining rights or limited representation rights[181] can also approach the Tripartite Panel, which has been set up to offer mediation services. This mediation is compulsory.[182] However, there is also a one-year limitation other than in the case of termination, in which case it is six months,[183] and legal representation is not allowed.[184]

226. In addition to that, there is the Tripartite Alliance for Dispute Management which provides mediation services for the lower end of the spectrum and the Singapore Mediation Centre, which provides mediation services for the higher end of the spectrum.

227. On the whole, mediation plays an important role when it comes to employment disputes.

---

181. *See* para. 236.
182. Section 30(J) of the Industrial Relations Act.
183. Section 30(G) of the Industrial Relations Act.
184. Section 30(H) of the Industrial Relations Act.

§2. Employment Claims Tribunal

228. The Employment Claims Tribunal provides a ready and inexpensive avenue for the resolution of employment disputes. However, there are various preconditions and limitations.

229. The first limitation is that the tribunal is only meant for certain types of statutory, contractual and/or wrongful dismissal claims. The general idea is for it to deal with the lower level, less complex claims.

230. Another limitation is that the claim amount cannot be more than SGD 20,000, other than claims involving unions in which it can be up to SGD 30,000. Importantly, claims must also first be preceded by mediation.

§3. Industrial Arbitration Court

231. Any dispute between the union and the employer can be mediated at the Ministry of Manpower. There is also the possibility of compulsory mediation by virtue of section 23 of the Industrial Relations Act. If mediation does not work, there is the possibility of arbitration under the Industrial Arbitration Court, including the possibility of compulsory arbitration. This is by virtue of section 31 of the Industrial Relations Act. As a matter of practice, the instances of compulsory arbitration have not been common, and even the instances of arbitration have not been that frequent. This is so as most disputes are amicably resolved via mediation.

Part II. Collective Labour Relations

Chapter 1. Trade Union and Employer Associations

§1. Background

232. The hallmark of industrial relations in Singapore is one of harmony. There is a strong tripartite relationship based on trust, and disputes are sought to be settled in a peaceful manner without resorting to industrial action. The system is one that has generally worked well as a matter of practice and one which aims to be constructive in nature. It may also be highlighted that Singapore has ratified the International Labour Organization's Right to Organize and Collective Bargaining Convention (No. 98).

233. On the other hand, Singapore has not ratified the International Labour Organization's Freedom of Association and Protection of the Right to Organize Convention (No. 87). This convention has probably not been ratified because the legislation relating to industrial relations in Singapore provides for various restrictions (highlighted below) in terms of the right to organize and collectively bargain. In addition, though the Constitution[185] guarantees the right to organize, this is subject to the right of Parliament to impose 'such restrictions as it considers necessary or expedient in the interest of the security of Singapore or any part thereof, public order or morality'.

§2. Definition of Trade Unions

234. Under section 2 of the Trade Unions Act, the term 'trade union' is defined to mean any association or combination of workmen or employers, whether temporary or permanent, whose principal object is to regulate relations between workmen and employers for all or any of the following purposes:

- to promote good industrial relations between workmen and employers;
- to improve the working conditions of workmen or enhance their economic and social status and
- to achieve the raising of productivity for the benefit of workmen, employers and the economy of Singapore,

185. Article 14(1)c of the Constitution of the Republic of Singapore.

and includes any federation of two or more trade unions.

§3. Registering, Running and Dissolving Trade Unions

235. In order to set up a union, one has to register the union. Section 8(1) of the Trade Unions Act provides that every union has to be registered within one month from the date it is established. Under section 9(1) of the Trade Unions Act, every application for registration has to be signed by at least seven members. However, the Registrar may refuse to register a trade union, and the grounds on which he may do so are set out in section 14 of the Trade Unions Act, and these include the situation where the rules of the trade union are unlawful, unreasonable or oppressive or where there is already an existing trade union in respect of that particular trade, occupation or industry, the idea behind the last restriction being not to have multiple unions thereby giving rise to rivalry and duplication of work. Even after the trade union is registered, the registration may be cancelled or withdrawn on various grounds as set out in section 15 of the Trade Unions Act. Such grounds include the situation where the trade union is being used for any unlawful purpose or for any purpose inconsistent with its objects or rules of the trade union.

236. In terms of the actual running a trade union, there are also detailed rules relating to matters such as the manner of holding of property, the usage of funds, the keeping of accounts and the submission of annual returns and these are set out in the Trade Unions Act as well as the Trade Union Regulations.

§4. Membership in Trade Unions

237. All employees can form trade unions. In fact, under the Employment Act[186] and the Industrial Relations Act,[187] an employee cannot be prevented from joining or setting up a trade union. Nonetheless, in relation to government employees and statutory board employees, there are some restrictions. In relation to government employees, pursuant to the Trade Unions (Government Officers – Exemption) Notification, they can form unions, but the membership in such trade unions has to be confined to persons employed by the government or certain specified boards or bodies. Nonetheless, the said notification also provides that members of the Singapore Police Force, the Civil Defence Force, the Singapore Armed Force and all officers of the Prisons Service cannot form unions. As for statutory board employees, while they too can form unions, section 29 of the Trade Unions Act provides that membership of such a trade union has to be confined exclusively to persons employed by such a board.

238. Foreign employees too can join unions, but they cannot take on management positions in the unions unless they obtain the prior written approval of the

186. Section 17 of the Employment Act.
187. Sections 79–82 of the Industrial Relations Act.

Minister of Manpower as provided in section 30 of the Trade Unions Act, the idea behind the restriction being that foreigners may not be familiar with the system of industrial relations in Singapore. Thus, for instance, it would be difficult to set up a union made up entirely for foreigners (such as one relating specifically to foreign domestic maids). Section 30 of the Trade Unions Act also provides that any person who is an undischarged bankrupt or who has been convicted by any court of criminal breach of trust, extortion or criminal intimidation, or any offence which, in the opinion of the Minister, renders him to be unfit to be an officer of a trade union, cannot be elected as an officer.

239. A distinction should be made between the executive and non-executive unions. Formally, one could not be formed to collectively represent the other. However, following recent amendments, a non-executive union can represent executive employees to carry out collective bargaining. However, even then, certain executive employees such as those in senior management are excluded. Another option for executive employees (which has existed for some time) is that, if there is a non-executive union representing employees of the employer, executive employees may join such a union just to get partial representation rights pursuant to section 30A of the Industrial Relations Act. If the section 30A route is taken, the non-executive union cannot collectively bargain for the executive employees. However, the non-executive union may individually help them negotiate with the employer or act on their behalf in relation to some specific matters such as dismissal. There is a definition in section 30A of who is an executive for this purpose so as to again exclude certain employees such as those in senior management.

240. Instead of joining non-executive unions, executives may form their own union. There are indeed such unions. However, they are not that common given that the number of members may be smaller, and it may be more difficult to sustain such a union as a result.

241. Yet another alternative for such executive employees is to join a union as a general branch member. If he does so, the union would not be able to collectively bargain for him or individually represent him or take action on their behalf. However, he may be able to get some general advice, and he would also be able to enjoy the social benefits (such as perhaps getting various shopping discounts and insurance coverage) of being a member of a union.

242. Currently, in Singapore, there about sixty-six employee trade unions and three employer-related unions or federations, and about 20% of the employees are unionized. The bulk, but not all, of the unions in Singapore are affiliated with the National Trade Unions Congress, which is the only federation of trade unions in Singapore. The National Trade Unions Congress has close links with the government, and by being affiliated with the National Trade Unions Congress, the unions which are affiliated share largely similar ideologies.

Chapter 2. Collective Bargaining

§1. The Process

243. The first step in the collective bargaining process is for the employer to recognize the trade union as provided in section 17 of the Industrial Relations Act. If the employer does not recognize the trade union, the matter may be brought to the Commissioner of Labour, who has the power to call for a secret ballot to see whether the majority of the employees entitled to vote are members of that particular trade union. If they are, then the employer has to grant recognition within three days. These matters are provided for in the Industrial Relations (Recognition of a Trade Union of Employees) Regulations.

244. Once recognition has been granted, either party may serve on the other a notice to negotiate on matters with the aim of arriving at the collective agreement as provided in section 18 of the Industrial Relations Act. However also, as provided in section 18 of the Industrial Relations Act, in Singapore, a trade union of employees cannot negotiate on the following matters:

(a) the promotion of any employee;
(b) the transfer of an employee within the organization provided that the transfer does not entail a change to the detriment of the employee in regard to his terms of employment;
(c) the employment of any person by the employer in the event of a vacancy;
(d) the termination or criteria for termination of the services of an employee by reason of redundancy or reorganization;
(e) the dismissal or reinstatement of any employee in circumstances in which section 35(3)[188] applies; and
(f) the assignment or allocation of duties to an employee which is not inconsistent with his terms of employment.

245. These matters are excluded as they are seen as prerogatives of the employer. If the trade union attempts to do so, it would be committing an offence.[189] Nonetheless, if the employer wants, he can negotiate on these issues with the union.

246. If a collective agreement cannot be reached, there is a possibility of mediation, including compulsory mediation.[190] Failure to observe an order of the Minister to go for mediation can result in the commission of an offence.[191]

---

188. This refers to the situation where the employee considers that he has been dismissed without just cause or reason. In such case, the employee may bring the matter to the union which can then bring the matter to the Minister of Manpower instead of directly negotiating with the employer.
189. Section 29 of the Industrial Relations Act.
190. Section 23 of the Industrial Relations Act.
191. *Ibid.*

§2. The Collective Agreement

247. The collective agreement will typically not apply to some employees, such as temporary employees or probationary employees. However, as for employees covered, the collective agreement will typically provide for many benefits such as retirement benefits, marriage leave, compassionate leave, study leave and various allowances. In addition, benefits that are normally given or which may be a statutory right under the Employment Act may be extended. For instance, there may be more days of annual leave, or there might be co-payment of medical expenses, whereas, under the Employment Act, the employer is only obliged to undertake the cost of the medical examination and not the cost of treatment.[192] It could also cover other matters such as salary ranges and the establishment of grievance procedures.

248. For a collective agreement to be binding, it has to be certified by the Industrial Arbitration Court.[193] The Industrial Arbitration Court may decide not to certify a collective agreement if it is of the view that it is against public interest or if the memorandum submitted does not set out satisfactorily or adequately all the terms of the agreement.[194]

249. There is also a maximum and minimum period of duration. The maximum is three years, and the minimum is two years.[195] There is a maximum so that the parties can consider the changed circumstances, and there is a minimum so that there is not too much disruption.

§3. Enforcement of the Collective Agreement

250. The collective agreement which is certified is legally binding and can be enforced by the employer or trade union or their successors.[196]

§4. Disputes Relating to the Collective Agreement

251. In relation to disputes relating to the interpretation of the collective agreement, the collective agreement would typically provide for reference to a referee.[197] If that does not work, there is a process of mediation, including compulsory mediation.[198] There is also the possibility of arbitration under the Industrial Arbitration Court.[199]

192. *See* para. 117.
193. Section 25 of the Industrial Relations Act.
194. *Ibid.*
195. *Ibid.*
196. Section 26 of the Industrial Relations Act.
197. Section 25 of the Industrial Relations Act.
198. Section 23 of the Industrial Relations Act.
199. Section 31 of the Industrial Relations Act.

Chapter 3. Strikes and Lockouts

252. There are three statutes governing strikes and lockouts in Singapore. They are the Trade Unions Act, the Trade Disputes Act and the Criminal Law (Temporary Provisions) Act.

§1. Trade Unions Act

253. Under section 27(15) of the Trade Unions Act, the term 'industrial action' is defined as the adoption of any practice, procedure or method in the performance of work that would result in a limitation on output or production in any occupation, service, trade, industry or business. Thus, even a 'go slow' action or 'work to rule' is likely to amount to industrial action.

254. However, before such industrial action can be carried out, the majority of the members of the trade union, who are affected, must approve of the action by means of a secret ballot.[200] This is to prevent a few militant members in the trade union from taking action on their own without the support of the others. Breach of this provision results in the commission of an offence.[201]

§2. Criminal Law (Temporary Provisions) Act

255. Under section 5 of the Criminal Law (Temporary Provisions) Act, the term 'strike' is defined as a 'cessation of work by a body of persons employed in any essential service acting in combination, or a concerned refusal or a refusal under a common understanding of a number of persons who are or who have been so employed to continue to work or to accept employment'. This definition seems narrower than that of the term 'industrial action' under the Trade Unions Act, in that, for instance, a 'go slow' action may not be covered.

256. Under section 6(1) of the Criminal Law Temporary Provisions, strike action is prohibited for the three essential services of water, gas and electricity. Breach of section 6(1) results in the commission of an offence.[202]

257. For other essential services, under section 6(2)a, the employer has to be informed at least fourteen days in advance. Breach of this provision results in the commission of an offence.[203] The reason for this to make the parties go for mediation or possibly arbitration once the fact that there is a dispute comes to light, in the hope that the dispute can be amicably resolved. The 'other essential services' covered are extensive and include banking services, broadcasting services, postal and

200. Section 27 of the Trade Unions Act.
201. *Ibid.*
202. Section 9 of the Criminal Law (Temporary Provisions) Act.
203. *Ibid.*

telecommunication services, port, dock and harbour services, public transport and air transport services, private and public health services, refuse or water collection services and services provided by the Immigration and Checkpoint Authority. In addition, under section 6(2)c of the Criminal Law (Temporary Provisions) Act, in relation to the other essential services, no strike shall take place during the pendency of proceedings, breach of which results in the commission of an offence. The reason behind this requirement is, again, to resolve disputes amicably without having to resort to industrial action.

Similar restrictions apply in relation to lockouts by the employer.[204]

§3. Trade Disputes Act

258. Under section 2 of the Trade Disputes Act, the term 'industrial action' means an act or omission by a body of persons employed in any trade or industry, acting in combination or under a common understanding, which would result in any limitation or restriction on, or delay in, the performance of any duties connected with their employment; or a strike, that is to say, the cessation of work by a body of persons employed in any trade or industry acting in combination, or a concerted refusal, or a refusal under a common understanding of a number of persons who are, or who have been so employed, to continue to work or to accept employment. Thus this definition is wide and can include, for instance, 'go slow' actions.

259. Under the Trade Disputes Act, certain forms of violence or intimidation during industrial action is prohibited.[205] The Trade Disputes Act also provides that industrial action is prohibited if it has any object other than the furtherance of a trade dispute.[206] Thus, for instance, it is not possible to strike against an unpopular government policy such as an increase in petrol prices. Further under the Trade Disputes Act, any form of industrial action is prohibited if it is in furtherance of a trade dispute of which the Industrial Arbitration Court has cognizance, the reason as mentioned above, being to encourage the resolution of disputes in a peaceful manner.[207] Breach of these provisions of the Trade Disputes Act results in the commission of the offence.[208]

Similar restrictions apply in relation to lockouts by the employer.[209]

§4. Relationship Between the Three Statutes

260. On any set of facts, it is possible for one or all three statutes to apply. The Trade Unions Act only applies to trade unions, but the other two statutes seem more general and can apply to non-unionized employees as well. Thus recently, when

204. Section 6 of the Criminal Law (Temporary Provisions) Act.
205. Section 9 of the Trade Disputes Act.
206. Section 3 of the Trade Disputes Act.
207. *Ibid.*
208. Section 5 of the Trade Disputes Act.
209. Section 3 of the Trade Disputes Act.

there was a strike by transport workers who were not members of a trade union, they were charged under the Criminal Law (Temporary Provisions) Act. However, other than this recent strike in 2012, Singapore has been strike free since 1986. As for lockouts by employers, there have been no such incidents for decades.

Chapter 4. Settlement of Industrial Conflicts

§1. Mediation

261. Mediation is strongly used in the resolution of industrial disputes. However, if one of the parties is not willing to go for mediation, as already mentioned, there is also the possibility of compulsory mediation.[210]

§2. Arbitration

262. In addition, if the matter is not resolved by mediation, reference may be made to the Industrial Arbitration Court. The grounds on which an application can be made to the Industrial Arbitration Court are set out in section 31 of the Industrial Relations Act. Under section 31 of the Industrial Relations Act, both parties can jointly make an application, or in some specific situations, either party may make an application. In addition, under section 31, it is possible for the Minister or the President of Singapore to make an application. Thus, there is a possibility of compulsory arbitration (though this has not been invoked often as a matter of practice) even if the parties do not want to go for arbitration. In this way, disputes are settled amicably without having to resort to industrial action.

263. It should also be highlighted that the Industrial Arbitration Court has to have regard to 'not only the interests of the persons immediately concerned, but to the interests of the community as a whole and in particular, the condition of the economy of Singapore'.[211] Further, the court has to act in accordance to 'equity, good conscience and substantial merits of the case, without regard to technicalities and legal forms'.[212] This is another example of Singapore trying to balance the interests of the employer with that of the employee as well as that of the general public. This makes the whole system very practical as well. Legal representation is also not allowed in the Industrial Arbitration Court,[213] the idea being that the presence of lawyers is more likely to hinder rather than aid the process.

264. Another interesting feature of arbitration is that, subject to some exceptions, there is tripartite representation in the Industrial Arbitration Court.[214] The arbitrating court is empowered to make awards when settling disputes.[215] Breach of an award is an offence.[216] The arbitrating court can also force compliance with the terms of the award.[217]

---

210. Section 23 of the Industrial Relations Act.
211. Section 34 of the Industrial Relations Act.
212. Section 60 of the Industrial Relations Act.
213. Section 64 of the Industrial Relations Act.
214. Section 3(2) read with ss 6(1) and 11(1) of the Industrial Relations Act.
215. Section 35 of the Industrial Relations Act.
216. Section 52 of the Industrial Relations Act.
217. Sections 56 and 57 of the Industrial Relations Act.

§3. PRACTICE

265. As a matter of practice, while disputes have been referred to the Industrial Arbitration Court, the vast number of disputes is settled amicably by mediation rather than by arbitration. The Ministry of Manpower also has a strong presence on the ground, facilitating and encouraging this process whenever disputes emerge.

266. It must also be highlighted that, on the whole, the system aspires to be fair to all the stakeholders concerned. If the system was not as such, it is doubtful whether industrial relations (or the political environment, for that matter) in Singapore would have turned out or continued to be generally peaceful and stable.

Selected Bibliography

Legislation

Singapore legislation, including that relating to employment, is available without charge at: http://statutes.agc.gov.sg/

Cases

Singapore and Malaysian cases, both reported and unreported, are available at http://www.lawnet.com.sg payment of a fee

Journal Articles

Chandran, Ravi. 'Bonuses and Other Payments in Employment Singapore'. *Academy of Law Journal* (2012): 338.

Chandran, Ravi. 'Dealing with Employee Crimes; Singapore'. *Academy of Law Journal* (2009): 35.

Chandran, Ravi. 'Privacy in Employment; Singapore'. *Journal of Legal Studies* (2000): 263.

Chandran, Ravi. 'Wage Cuts and the Law; Singapore'. *Academy of Law Journal* (1999): 211.

Lee Tsen-Ta, Jack. 'Workplace Sexual Harassment in Singapore'. *Singapore Academy of Law Journal* (1999): 27.

Websites

Employment-Related Information is available at: http://www/mom.gov.sg/.

The Tripartite Alliance for Fair Employment Practices is available at: http://www.tafep.sg/.

Information Relating to the Central Provident Fund Board is available at: http://mycpf.cpf.gov.sg/.

Information Relating to Workfare Supplement is available at: http://mycpf.gov.sg/Members/Gen-Info/WIS/WISSheme.

Information Relating to the Industrial Arbitration Court is available at: http://www.iac.gov.sg/.

Information on the Singapore Mediation Centre is available at: http://www.mediation.com.sg/.

The Industrial Arbitration Court is available at: http://www.iac.gov.sg/.

The National Trade Unions Congress is available at: http://www.ntuc.org.sg/.

The Ministry of Manpower is available at: http://www.mom.gov.sg/.

Selected Bibliography

Books

Barker, Deborah. *A Guide to Termination of Employment in Singapore.* LexisNexis. 2008.
Chandran, Ravi. *Employment Law in Singapore.* Lexis Nexis. 2019.
Chandran, Ravi. *Employment Act.* Lexis Nexis. 2009.
Chandran, Ravi. *Work Injury Compensation Act.* Lexis Nexis. 2010.
Haut, Tan Chwee. *Employment Relations in Singapore.* Pearson. 2002.

Index

The numbers here refer to paragraph numbers.

Index

www.ingramcontent.com/pod-product-compliance
Ingram Content Group UK Ltd.
Pitfield, Milton Keynes, MK11 3LW, UK
UKHW020150290926
15471UKWH00004B/797

9 789403 536859